P9-CCR-142

Judith
November 1990
Kinston, North Carolina

Entertaining
With Southern Living®

Entertaining With Southern Living

MARGARET CHASON AGNEW

Oxmoor House

Copyright 1990 by Oxmoor House, Inc.
Book Division of Southern Progress Corporation
P.O. Box 2463 Birmingham, Alabama 35201

All rights reserved. No part of this book may be reproduced in any form or by any means without the prior written permission of the publisher, excepting brief quotes in connection with reviews written specifically for inclusion in a magazine or newspaper.

Library of Congress Catalog Number: 90-61593
ISBN: 0-8487-0780-X

Manufactured in the United States of America
First Printing 1990

Executive Editor: Ann H. Harvey
Production Manager: Jerry Higdon
Associate Production Manager: Rick Litton
Art Director: Bob Nance

Entertaining With Southern Living®

Senior Foods Editor: Margaret Chason Agnew
Assistant Foods Editor: Julie Fisher
Copy Editor: Mary Ann Laurens
Editorial Assistants: Pam Beasley Bullock, Leigh Anne Roberts
Production Assistant: Theresa Beste
Test Kitchen Director: Vanessa Taylor Johnson
Test Kitchen Home Economists: Angie C. Neskaug, Christina A. Pieroni, Kathleen Royal,
   Gayle Hays Sadler, Paula N. Saunders, Jill Wills
Senior Photographer: Jim Bathie
Photo Stylist: Kay E. Clarke
Designer: Faith M. Nance
Illustrator: Stacy Claire Boyd

Cover: *The front porch of a country farm home is the setting for this Southern Vegetable Dinner (page 127).*
Back cover: *(clockwise from top right) Silver Anniversary Dinner (page 115), Lunch for the Ladies (page 157), and Southern Vegetable Dinner (page 127).*
Page 2: *An antique lace cloth and your favorite china and crystal can be combined for lovely outdoor dining.*

To find out how you can receive *Southern Living* magazine, write to *Southern Living*®,
P.O. Box 830119, Birmingham, AL 35283.

Contents

Menus for Entertaining

Foreword

For over 25 years, the foods staff of *Southern Living* has played a leading role in furthering Southern hospitality. Each month, cooks across the South turn to the magazine's food pages for recipes and entertaining ideas. For eight years, I was a part of that team and helped collect and assemble the entertaining features. I spent a great deal of time talking with hosts and hostesses and visiting in their homes while parties were being photographed.

It was on just such an occasion when I began to envision *Entertaining With Southern Living*. I realized it should be a book that would stimulate thoughts and themes for party decorating ideas and party locations. I also believed it should be a practical book—with more people electing to entertain at home, the recipes and ideas needed to be stylish, yet realistic and achievable.

The actual book includes all that I originally dreamed of and more. It is a complete guide to home entertaining. The menus have been created to serve gatherings of from two to twelve guests. And busy cooks will find that the menus can be adjusted to suit their needs. For example, rather than baking the suggested bread or making homemade pickles, these items may be purchased ready-made. For those who want to serve the correct wine or beverage, we have, when appropriate, made suggestions that we hope you will find exciting and pleasurable. Dr. David J. Black, wine consultant and owner of the Birmingham Wine Shop, carefully sought the ideal marriages of wine and food.

The contributions of photo stylists Kay Clarke and Marjorie Johnston set the stage for this book. Many mornings I found them clipping and arranging flowers or in someone's garden, moving chairs to where the sunlight was "just right." And photographers Jim Bathie and Beth Maynor were always willing to go the extra mile, including patiently waiting for thunderstorms to pass.

The food presented in this book is mouth-watering and beautiful—partially because the recipes were painstakingly selected, but mostly because the skilled test kitchen staff of Oxmoor House paid close attention to detail and presentation. Kathleen Royal, Angie Neskaug, and Jill Wills, location photography home economists, produced some artful masterpieces, even when they found themselves working in unfamiliar kitchens or outside on a lawn.

Thanks are due to these and all the other people who helped make the book a reality. I hope this book enables you to spend many happy occasions with your family and friends.

Margaret Chason Agnew

Planning the Party

Planning a party should be fun; it gives you a chance to express your personality and to share your most treasured possessions with guests.

9

Southern Entertaining Today

Southern cooks are, by nature, warm, creative people. They seem to be born knowing how to make guests feel welcome, and they have a special talent for always being able to stir up something wonderful to eat. In the old South, cooks probably never thought of it as "entertaining," but they always had lots of "company." The true country cook never dreamed of having a dinner party, but she was always ready to share food she had prepared with others. Few Sundays passed that she didn't host relatives or church members to a memorable feast of fried chicken, baked ham, an assortment of fresh vegetables, fist-size biscuits, layer cakes, and prize-winning pies. And the amazing part was that this sumptuous meal was prepared and served with natural ease and comfort—traits still admired by modern cooks.

The new Southerner appreciates all that is modern but still relishes old traditions—a delightful combination. We still love to grill outdoors, and, with air conditioning, we can enjoy a dinner party on the hottest August evening. We still love our garden-fresh vegetables, but we've

This Southern kitchen is tailor-made for entertaining. It is spacious enough to allow guests to get involved with the actual food preparation or to sit back and join in the conversation.

learned that they retain more nutrients and flavor if they aren't cooked for hours. Today we see a continuing interest in health, so many cooks watch what they eat all week in order to splurge on their favorite foods on the weekend. These same cooks also want convenience, so the new Southern kitchen is often equipped with a microwave oven, food processor, pasta machine, and espresso maker. All this has led us to discover the joy of combining the old and the new with a creative touch.

We new Southerners love to "entertain." Our warm, generous hospitality has become a national phenomenon. All across the country, hosts and hostesses are seeking the secrets for successful entertaining that Southerners have always known. We like to make our guests feel welcome by seating them at a pretty dining table and satisfying their appetites with the best we have to offer. While our meals are not necessarily lavish, we do strive to serve good, attractive food. Our carefully planned menus are a pleasing blend of the old and the new. Most important, Southerners base their special entertaining style on a simple principle— please guests by making them feel a part of a warm, personal, happy occasion.

Occasions for Entertaining

When is it appropriate to entertain? Specific occasions may vary—a poolside supper to celebrate a birthday, a relaxed weekend lunch with neighbors, a sunset picnic for the dinner club members, a sophisticated dinner party to honor a business associate—but each event can fulfill the basic Southern requirement of being an intimate social affair.

Birthdays and holidays are obvious opportunities to throw a party, but there is no need for the occasion to always be so obvious. And entertaining doesn't always have to be centered around a complete meal. Other possibilities for entertaining include breakfasts, coffees, brunches, luncheons, afternoon teas, cocktail parties, dinner parties, supper parties, dinner dances, dessert parties—the list goes on and on. Always keep in mind your interests and intent. For example, do you want a huge, blow-out feast for hundreds or a simple gathering of a few couples?

Nowadays, entertaining provides an opportunity to express yourself and be creative. One hostess may enjoy having a family picnic beside a bubbling brook on some of Grandmother's country quilts. Another may prefer bringing out all her finest crystal and china for a dinner party before the symphony. A wine connoisseur may get a kick out of sharing dinner and his latest wine acquisition right in his wine cellar. With a little thought, creative people can always come up with a reason and a place to entertain.

Choosing the Location

Almost any attractive location that suggests a particular mood can be a party site. You can create a romantic setting by placing a frilly cloth on a table in a pretty garden that contains a vine-covered trellis or a fountain with a musical trickle of water. Or stir up your desire for adventure by packing an entire meal in huge laundry hampers and transporting it to a deserted clover-filled pasture or to the local zoo.

No doubt there are as many good sites for entertaining as there are personalities. Invariably, some of the best places to entertain are right at home. Try placing a table in front of the living room fireplace. Or clear off a corner of the front porch and dress up a table with all of your lacy linens. Try draping the interior of your garage with sheets to hide the clutter; fill the empty floor space with tables or even a band.

An ordinary wooden deck can be transformed into a floating star by outlining it with votive candles. Consider having a tent installed across your backyard for a large dinner or dance party. And stretch your creativity by turning your basement into a fabulous halloween spook house.

Formal versus Informal

In recent years, changing lifestyles have resulted in almost all rules for entertaining being bent or even broken. But, when we examine the vast possibilities for different types of parties, it's clear that events still fall into two

The idea of planning an important dinner party may be overwhelming, but you will gain great pleasure when you survey the beautifully appointed table.

major categories—formal and informal. Most formal events are still sit-down affairs, with the host and hostess being particularly mindful of correct etiquette. However, informal get-togethers open up the world of stand-up cocktail parties, serve-yourself buffets, casual brunches, small lunches, and impromptu dinners.

Even if the idea of giving a formal party doesn't appeal to you, it's a good idea to be familiar with how it's done. You never know when you may find yourself in a situation where formal dining is the preferred choice. And, surprisingly, there are times when a formal meal can provide a nice change and a rewarding success for the hostess, for this occasion allows her the chance to show off a grand meal and a beautifully appointed table.

Try not to think of formal meals as being stiff and uncomfortable. Instead, think of them as a time to leisurely savor the food and enjoy the company. Formal occasions also offer guests a chance to engage in deep, extended

Always try to offer appetizers in an interesting manner. You might consider serving them from a small table placed in the foyer.

conversations and an opportunity to form interesting acquaintances and lasting friendships.

A formal meal should begin by having a butler or waiter, dressed in black and white or gray and white, answer the door. Coats are taken and guests are shown into the living room where they are greeted by the host and hostess. A cocktail period follows with dinner being announced by the waiter a half hour later.

The host ushers in and seats the female guest of honor to his right, followed by the other guests, with the hostess and male guest of honor entering last. The table should be set with impeccable appointments of fine china, crystal, and silver. Any candles should be glowing before guests arrive in the dining area. If the first course is soup or oysters, it should be on the table when guests are seated. However, if the first course is fish or salad, only the service plates should be present; the actual dish will be served by the waiter once guests have removed their napkins from the table.

The waiter will serve and remove all food with his left hand, from the guest's left side. All beverages, including wines, will be served and removed by the waiter from the guest's right side, with the right hand, being careful not to collide with any of the other beverage glasses.

When serving a formal meal, a waitress should follow behind the waiter with any additional sauces or breads. Before dessert is served, it is preferable for the table to be cleared of plates, salt and pepper, place cards, and even crumbs. Coffee is not offered at the table but is served in the living room.

If the occasion lends itself to informal-style entertaining, then relax! Just make sure each guest is welcomed and introduced to enough of the other guests so that no one feels ill at ease. The first course can be served as an appetizer anywhere you think appropriate—on the living room coffee table or on the den sofa table. Appetizers can even be served from a bookcase or a piano, if they are easy to reach. Some hostesses like to offer guests a variety of small appetizers, serving each appetizer in a different room or area of the house.

For informal entertaining, your guests can be seated at the dining table, on pillows around the den television set, or almost any other inviting spot. A conveniently located buffet makes serving easier, but for very informal parties the kitchen counter can double as a buffet. Another excellent aid is a rolling cart.

Wine is generally served as soon as the appetizers appear and is usually offered by the host. He should keep in mind to fill glasses no more than half full because guests do not want to overdo early in the evening. In addition, a second wine may be offered with the main course.

An informal buffet will often get off to a better start if the hostess helps fill the dinner plates for several of the guests. This allows guests to see what goes with what and the expected portion size. Of course, guests should always be encouraged, but not pressed, to go back for seconds. When a guest does rise to return for seconds, he should place his napkin in the chair, not on the table.

Sometimes at an informal party, it is nice if the dessert can be served in a different part of the house. If dinner is served in the dining room, the hostess may offer dessert on the deck or porch or even in the game room while some of the guests play pool. Many modern kitchens have eat-in areas, and these provide the perfect spot for an intimate ending to a meal.

Guests can, and should, offer to help clean up, but under no circumstances should the cleanup begin until everyone is through eating. It is also worth pointing out that the cleanup shouldn't begin until it is really time for everyone to go home, because nothing runs guests off like the anxious clatter of dirty dishes.

Getting Organized

There are many ways to become a calm and collected hostess, and making a list and having a definite game plan is the first step toward achieving this. A list lets you know exactly where you stand at any given moment before or after guests arrive. And carefully laid plans are by far the best ensurance for a pleasant entertaining experience. For worry-free entertaining, it is best to start with a master list of the following major preliminary questions:

1. What is the reason for the event?
2. Where will the event be held? Will the meal be served indoors, outdoors, at home, or in a rented facility?
3. Is there a particular date or season when the event should take place?
4. What time of day or night is most appropriate for the event?
5. Should the occasion be informal or formal?
6. How many guests should be invited?
7. What type of food and beverage is most appropriate to serve?
8. What is the budget for this event?
9. What decorations are appropriate for this event?
10. Is music or some other type of entertainment needed?

In making these initial decisions, plan as far in advance as possible. The dates for some occasions—large weddings, anniversaries, and graduations—can be planned as much as a year in advance. Invitations for formal occasions can be sent out three or four weeks in advance. Invitations to informal dinner parties can be made by phone or a note, one or two weeks in advance.

The guest list can be made up of family members, club members, long-time friends, co-workers, or any group of people that you think would make an interesting, harmonious mix. If hosting a party in honor of someone else, it's best to let the guest of honor help prepare the guest list; in that case, many of the names may be unfamiliar to you, so be sure to determine the correct names and spellings in advance. Also keep in mind the amount of space available and match the number of guests to the space.

When considering the budget, always start with estimates of the amount of liquor and food to be served, the items to be rented, servants' fees, music or other entertainment expenses, and floral and other decorative expenses. When you work your way through the budget the first time, start off with your "dream" budget; then work backwards until you find yourself within your actual budget. Remember, the amount of money you spend need not dictate how much fun your guests will have. A creative hostess can find many inexpensive ways to delight and surprise her guests.

Decorations and entertainment help set the stage for your party. It's good to get into the habit of keeping a

Whatever the event, a party goods store can help you set the stage, focus on a theme, and create a festive mood without a large expense or a lot of effort.

To help you keep an accurate record of all your party details, write everything down on a notepad, or use a form such as The Party Planner on page 240.

current file folder of party ideas, themes, decorations, and menus that you think your friends would enjoy. Any time you hear an exciting band, a talented pianist, or a string trio or quartet, put their name and phone number in the file. Depending on the event and the size of your budget, try to select flowers, decorations, and music that best reflect your personal style and the mood you want to set.

If you entertain often, it's a good idea to keep accurate records of parties in a notebook or on file cards. These records should note all the information from the preliminary list, plus the names of guests, what food was served, flowers used, any special seating arrangements, and what dress or outfit you wore. Try to include a sentence or two about

the menu, being sure to note what worked, what was a problem to prepare or serve, and what could have been made ahead. If a recipe was outstanding, be sure to make a copy of it or write down where it came from so that you can refer to it the next time. It is also important to note whether you were particularly pleased with the florist, the servers, and the musicians.

Hiring the Party Staff

After you have decided on a potential menu, think about how much help will be needed to allow the party or dinner to flow smoothly. There are many different kinds of assistants you can turn to—caterers, butlers, waiters and waitresses, bartenders, kitchen helpers, and parking valets.

Caterers can provide a variety of services from doing virtually everything to simply preparing the appetizers or a special dessert. When interviewing a caterer, be sure he or she listens carefully to all your plans and takes notes. It's best if the person selected can actually visit your party or dinner site and look it over ahead of time. Discuss all the specifics of the menu and make your budget, or price range, perfectly clear. The best way to find a good caterer is by asking friends who have had parties you particularly enjoyed what caterers they used.

To find the rest of the entertaining staff, ask friends or hire through an agency that specializes in household personnel. Also, check with club managers, restaurants, hotels, or the local college employment office. One of the best sources of helpers may be your own children and their friends. Unemployed college students usually make enthusiastic, animated servers.

Be sure to interview prospective waiters and bartenders in person beforehand. Ask

Select an entertaining staff that is neat, polite, and enjoyable to have around. They should also be cooperative and follow your instructions.

them about other parties where they have worked so that you can get an idea of their experience. You will want to make sure the prospective staff is neat, pleasant looking, courteous, understanding, and congenial.

As a general rule, you will need one experienced bartender for every 50 guests. It would be nice to have a bartender when you are having a small dinner party, but it's not essential. It would also be convenient, even at a small party of six to eight guests, to have a kitchen helper to do such chores as rinse dishes and make coffee. But anytime you have a dinner party of 10 or 12 guests, especially if it is a formal occasion, the need for extra help becomes more pressing. For a seated dinner with 12 guests, depending on your budget, you may need a waiter and a bartender or two waiters: one who can double as bartender before and after the meal and one who can serve appetizers and attend to the general needs of the guests. Both can clean up afterwards.

If a large at-home party or dinner is planned, and you realize parking space will be limited or congested, then the services of an off-duty policeman and a parking valet may be necessary. Check with your local police department to see if they can advise you and offer their services. In some cases, it may be possible to have cars parked in the parking lot of a nearby church or shopping mall or a vacant lot; guests could be whisked to the party site in a courtesy bus or van. Buses and vans usually can be rented from local automobile dealers or car rental agencies.

When dealing with hired staff, it is best to determine specifically the method of payment and the hours you expect them to work. Pay by the hour and tip for a job well done to ensure that their help is likely to be available next time they are needed. Always pay the helpers as soon as they have completed their duties. However, from the start, make it clear that you do not consider the job completed until the kitchen and dining areas are back to normal. Prepare individual pay envelopes ahead of time and have these ready to pass out.

Bartenders are typically busy when a party begins. They should have experience in assembling a bar and mixing drinks to fill requests quickly.

Emphasize that there should be no smoking or drinking in the presence of guests.

It is a good idea to post a copy of the menu in the kitchen. Along with the menu, post a time schedule reminding the help when appetizers are to be served, when the main course is to be served, and so forth. Some hostesses feel more comfortable reviewing with the staff a list of etiquette reminders such as these listed below:

1. All food is served and removed with the left hand from the left side of the guest.
2. All beverages are served and removed from the right side with the right hand. Be careful not to collide with other beverage glasses.
3. Never pick up a glass by placing your hand over the top of the glass.
4. Try to refill coffee cups and glasses without removing them from the table.
5. Keep a napkin in your left hand to wipe drips from coffee or water pitchers.
6. Never stack or scrape plates in the presence of the guests.
7. Remove salt, pepper, butter, and excess silver from the table after the main course is cleared away.
8. Above all, smile; be courteous and accommodating.

Discuss duties and appropriate dress with the help ahead of time so that they know exactly what is expected of them. Appropriate summer uniforms for bartenders, butlers, waiters, and parking valets consist of a white jacket or black vest, starched white shirt, and black bow tie. Black trousers, socks, and black shoes complete the outfit. Winter attire is similar, but a black jacket can be substituted. Waitresses should wear a gray or black uniform and perhaps a starched white apron.

A good bartender should be able to set up before a party in about an hour, and a waiter or waitress will need about 30 to 45 minutes to familiarize himself or herself with the kitchen and dining layout. On the day of the event, about 30 minutes before guests arrive, gather the staff and answer all last-minute questions. Specify again where garbage bags should be placed, what can go in the dishwasher, what must be washed by hand, and what to do with dirty linen.

Remember—entertaining should be pleasurable for both you and your guests. Try to relax; if the host or hostess continually jumps up and down or rushes to and from the kitchen this will make guests anxious and uncomfortable.

Always try to allow yourself time to wind down before guests are due. Keep a pad of paper close by so that you can jot down last-minute chores. If you have small children, engage a babysitter ahead of time. Make sure the sitter arrives early and gets the children bathed and fed before the party.

After doing all you can to plan and organize for your party, do not be alarmed if an accident does happen. Just accept that mistakes can be part of the fun and that everyone understands. Do all you can in advance; then settle back and let the help do what they have been hired to do—present the smoothest, most enjoyable party possible.

1526 Oak
Dallas, Texas 76102

You are invited...
...honoring Lauren L...
...th, 17th...
...452-7623

check one:
☐ - Yes! We SHELL attend.
☐ - Sorry Charli...

CHARLI...

Come Sea

Saturday, September 23
8:30 pm
3101 Cliff Road – A2
Birmingham, Alabama

O'Fishal Dress: Under Sea Costume

...Supper Club
invites you for
Cocktails and Dinner
Saturday, July 24
7 o'clock in the evening
...2. Old Leeds Road

Cas...

DINE AND DANCE

Friday, May 13th
7:30
Penthouse ~ Summit Club

Eugie and Lucian Minor

Black Tie

Please Come to a Party

for: Heidi and Julius
on: Thursday evening, January 11th
8 o'clock
at: The Winfrey Hotel

r.s.v.p. by Dec...
252 49...

Date: Friday evening, June 10
Time: 7:30 pm
Jill and Jay Patton
29 Ormoor Rd.

Please Come For a dinner party

Casual

Please join us for
Cocktails and Buffet
at seven pm
on Saturday, July 16
2913 Redmont Road
Birmingham

Jennifer and Bill Kessler

What is everyone whispering about?
haven't you heard about the party?
What Party?
IT'S ONLY THE MOST FABULOUS PARTY OF THE YEAR!!!
You'll be there... won't you?
Why I wouldn't miss it for the world!

Please Come For: Cocktails & Dinner
Place: 2960 Chickasaw Rd.
Date: Friday, June 12
Time: 8:00 pm

Liz and Jonathan
invite you to cel...
their Engageme...
Saturday, October...
8:00 p.m.
...East 80th Street
Houston, Tx

...d M...
...2 R...
...Road
...Tennessee
38

RSVP

Let the Party Begin

Invitations are the preview to the party. A cleverly designed invitation will spark enthusiasm for the coming event.

19

Invitations and Responses

The party begins the moment the guests receive their invitations. The invitation can be viewed as the preview to the party; it gives guests a chance to peek into the future and sample the fun of the occasion. It also gives them all the necessary information—the date, time, place, type of party or the occasion, names of the hosts, and name and phone number or address to respond to, if needed.

The way invitations are presented has a lot to do with how excited guests will be about attending. A bright, clever invitation is hard to resist; it makes the receiver think the party can't be missed because it is sure to be fun. Invitations to informal occasions can be imaginative and creative. You can make your own invitations in black and white and have copies printed; add bright slashes of color to liven them up. Some people even design an invitation consisting of a special gift that is hand-delivered to the guest's home. Informal invitations can be sent two weeks in advance. But when a get-together is spontaneous, a verbal invitation can be issued over the telephone.

Formal events demand a more sophisticated invitation. These should always be handwritten or engraved in black ink on white or cream-colored cards with matching envelopes. These invitations should be written in third person and mailed two weeks in advance. If a response is indicated, a handwritten note on personalized white or cream-colored stationery should be sent by the recipient.

If an invitation indicates that a response is desired, then be sure to contact the hostess as soon as possible.

When "regrets only" appears on an invitation, it means a guest responds only if he cannot attend. Anytime R.S.V.P. appears, a reply of either acceptance or regret is required. If an invitation is issued that requires a response from the guest, then you should be sure that someone is available to answer the phone; an answering machine could also help. If you need to calculate the quantity of food to prepare, but guests still haven't responded, do not hesitate to call and ask if they plan to attend. But even after you have received the responses, remember there will probably be a few last-minute cancellations due to illness or other unforeseen circumstances.

The following are examples of engraved formal dinner invitations:

Mr. and Mrs. Edward Walker
request the pleasure of your company
at dinner
on Friday, May the Fifth
at seven o'clock
243 Stratford Road

R.S.V.P.

Mr. and Mrs. Robert Cox
request the pleasure of
Mr. and Mrs. Bentley Anderson's
company at dinner
on Friday, May the Fifth
at eight o'clock
to meet Mr. and Mrs. Winston Callaway
R.S.V.P.
1510 Caraway Drive

A handwritten informal dinner invitation:

Dinner
Friday, March 23, 8 P.M.
Mrs. Hackney Smith
R.S.V.P.
62 North Manor Lane

A handwritten acceptance note to a formal dinner:

Mr. and Mrs. Frederick Williams
accept with pleasure
the kind invitation of
Mr. and Mrs. Edward Walker
to dine
on Friday, the fifth of May
at seven o'clock

Handwritten acceptance notes to an informal dinner:

We accept with pleasure for
the 23rd at eight
Mary

Would love to come Friday
at eight
Janice

A handwritten regret note to a formal dinner:

> *Mr. and Mrs. Mitchell White*
> *regret exceedingly*
> *that because of a previous engagement*
> *they will be unable to accept*
> *Mr. and Mrs. Walker's*
> *kind invitation for the fifth of May*

A handwritten regret note to an informal dinner:

> *So very sorry we*
> *can't join you and*
> *Hack on the 23rd—*
> *we will be out of town.*
> *Susan*

Sometimes an invitation will indicate how guests should be attired. It seems this varies somewhat in different areas of the South. But generally, if an invitation says "black tie," it means formal wear—tuxedoes with black bow tie for the men and long gowns or elegant cocktail dresses for the ladies. After 6:00 p.m., parties tend to be dressy. But, unless "black tie" appears on the invitation, men should wear dark suits and ties, and ladies should wear dressy dresses.

A thank-you note or phone call to the hostess following a party is a nice, impressive gesture. Some may feel that our modern society is too busy to follow through with this practice, but a brief, handwritten note or phone call commenting on the food, decorations, and thoughtfulness of the hostess should still be considered a necessity. If the dinner or party was very large, keep in mind that a barrage of phone calls could be worrisome to the hostess. In this case, a short thank-you note would definitely be more appropriate.

Accommodating Guests

Be certain that a warm, special greeting awaits guests upon arrival at the front door. At informal dinners and parties you may greet guests yourself or delegate the job to

Formal black-tie attire should only be worn after six o'clock in the evening.

Place cards can be a convenience to the hostess who is serving more than six or eight guests. The cards can be used on formal or informal tables.

Other methods can also be employed to help guests get acquainted. For example, ask each guest, when he or she arrives, to try to find the guest with the birthday closest to his own or possibly the guest or guests with the same number of children. You could even pass out party favors such as hats or balloons and have each guest find another guest with the matching hat or balloon.

When the actual time for an informal dinner nears, the hostess should announce that dinner will be served in 10 to 15 minutes. This gives guests a chance to freshen up. When it is actually time to head into the dining room, the hostess should lead the female guests into the dining room with the men following, and the host should enter last.

The seating at formal and informal dinners is basically the same. The host and hostess are seated opposite each other, usually at opposite ends of the table, with the hostess at the end nearest the kitchen area. To the right of the host is the female guest of honor, and to the right of the hostess is the male guest of honor. To the host's left is placed the next most important female guest and to the hostess' left, the next most important male guest.

Some guests may object to the use of place cards, but the fact remains that at formal dinners place cards are the best way for getting people to sit where you feel they are most likely to enjoy themselves. Place cards can also be used to encourage guests to become acquainted with each other. If it doesn't really matter where guests sit during dinner, by all means, let each guest select his or her own seat and dining partner.

There was a time when the hostess was supposed to take the lead in orchestrating table conversation. She talked

one of your friends, but the hostess should always be one of the first people the guest sees. Once guests are inside, make sure someone is assigned to show them where to store their coats and purses. If there is a special guest or a guest of honor, he or she should be positioned near the host or hostess so that he or she can be introduced to other guests.

Introductions should always be handled with the less important or younger person being introduced to the more important or elder person. For example, you would probably want to introduce your guest of honor, Tom, to a guest by saying, "Tom, I'd like you to meet Susan," or "Tom, I'd like to present my daughter, Susan." At very formal parties, a butler or waiter should announce the arrival of each guest at the door. If your guest of honor is coming from out of town and will be unacquainted with most of the guests, you might want to send him a list of the guests' names with a bit of information about each ahead of time.

Getting guests to mingle is often a challenge. You can help by providing name tags on a tray near the front door.

to the guest of honor the first half of the meal, then turned to direct the conversation to the gentleman on her left during the second half of the meal. Guests at the table were expected to do the same. But today, it is preferable for the hostess and the guests to talk to those seated on each side and across from them throughout the meal.

Upon completion of the dinner, the hostess should rise and indicate where coffee is to be served. The English prefer for men to remain at the dining table or to retire to the library or den. But a more modern style is for the men and women to enjoy coffee or liqueurs together.

When it is time to leave a dinner or party, a guest should never feel that a lengthy explanation is necessary. He may simply seek out the hostess and say that he is sorry to leave and has had an enjoyable time. The host or hostess should then accompany the guest to the front door.

Anyone who has entertained frequently has probably had the undesirable experience of having a guest who does not want to go home linger at the party. The best solution for this is to begin cleaning up the room and gathering up glasses and plates. If this doesn't spur the lingering guest out the door, then tell him politely how much you have enjoyed his company, but that you think you are ready to call it a night. Then ask if you can see him to the door or offer to call a cab to take him home.

Calling a cab for a guest may seem a little aggressive or rude, and should be done only when necessary. However, it is recommended that a host or hostess be willing to call a cab for a guest who has had too much alcohol to drink. Anytime you have invited a guest who may be considered a problem drinker, try to keep an eye on how much alcohol he consumes, and, if necessary, call a cab for him or ask a friend to drive him home.

Serving Arrangements

There are many different styles for serving food at a dinner party, but remember that the style of meal service you follow will help set the tone for the dinner. You may select American, European or formal, English, family, apartment or plate, or buffet service.

In American style, the table is completely set before guests are seated. Serving dishes of food are placed on the table or on a sideboard, and each dish is passed around the table until everyone has been served. Dessert may be brought in from the kitchen on individual dessert dishes, or it may be passed at the table as were the other courses.

European or formal service means that servants offer food to each guest and that no serving dishes appear on the table. When guests are seated, there is a cover or service plate at each place. Sequentially through the courses of the formal meal, plate replaces plate through the serving of the entrée or salad course, if the salad follows the entrée. The table is then cleared and dessert is served.

Originally, English service was only slightly less formal than European service. Platters of food and dinner plates were brought to the table by servants and placed in front of the host and hostess; the host carved and placed the meat on the dinner plate, and the hostess served the vegetables. A servant then took the plates from the host, to the hostess, then to the guests. Now it is more common for the plates simply to be passed by hand from the host, to the hostess, and back to the guests.

Family service is a variation of English service. Serving containers of meat and vegetables and a stack of dinner plates are placed in front of the host or hostess. The dinner plates are filled and then passed by hand until all guests have been served. Salad and dessert may be served in the same manner. This style service is best used when the group is small because it takes longer to get everyone served. The hostess often performs the duty of waiting on the table and taking dishes to and from the kitchen.

In apartment or plate service, plates are filled in the kitchen and placed on the table just before guests sit down. This type of service is used often at modern dinner parties because it allows the hostess control of the portion and presentation of the food on the plate. Serving a large number of plates is time consuming, so it is best to use this style service for small dinner parties. Originally used where the kitchen and dining areas were small, as in an apartment, this service is often used today simply to control the appearance and portions of food. The plates can be taken to the table by a servant or the hostess.

The most popular style of meal service, especially for large groups, is buffet service. A buffet can be set up on a dining table or other suitable surface, such as a chest, kitchen counter, or sideboard, that will accommodate a stack of dinner plates and serving dishes of food. Since the guests serve themselves, the buffet must be arranged carefully and logically.

When setting up a buffet table, the prime consideration should be traffic flow. Placement should allow easy circulation before, during, and after the meal. Proximity to the kitchen is important so that serving dishes may be replenished with ease. If the main dish is to be served over rice, the rice should come first in line. Dressings and sauces should be placed close to the dish they complement. Desserts may be served at one end of the buffet or placed on a serving cart and served after the guests have completed the main course. Beverages can be placed on a side table or served from a tray after the guests are seated.

Guests are invited to serve themselves at the buffet and dine according to the arrangements of the hostess. The

This buffet table is arranged so that guests can move around the table freely and serve themselves.

hostess of a buffet dinner may plan for guests to dine at a table that is fully set except for the dinner plate, or she may provide individual trays that hold the plate and beverage; then the guests can place the trays on their laps. Sometimes the arrangement made for buffet dining is simply to have a place where the guests can sit comfortably and set down their beverage; they are to eat from a plate held in the hand or placed on the lap.

If dining from a buffet, it is not necessary for all the guests to be served before those already seated start eating, though two or more guests usually form a group and eat together. After a casual, sit-where-you-may buffet meal is completed, guests should return their dirty dishes to the buffet table; the dishes will then be cleared to the kitchen. Dessert is brought in and is served from the buffet table or offered from a tray.

Example of a buffet arranged on a sideboard. In this case, the flatware, glassware, and napkins are already placed on the table for guests:

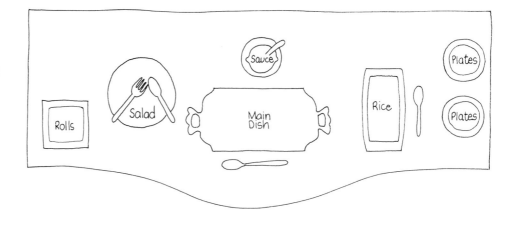

Example of a conveniently arranged buffet so that guests can proceed around the table:

Example of a buffet arranged so that guests can proceed in double rows from end to end. Beverages can be placed on a side table or served from a tray:

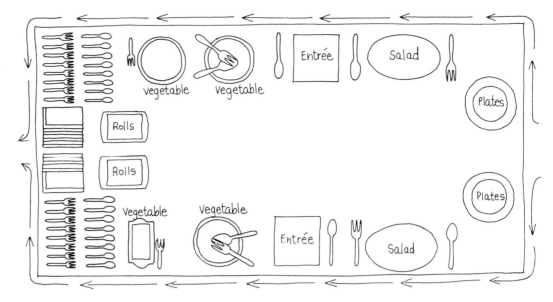

Setting the Table

Setting the table, like planning the menu, gives the hostess a chance to be creative by coordinating colors and combining decorative objects. But a more important consideration than aesthetics should be the workability of the table setting. Concern for the comfort of the guests should be foremost in the mind of the hostess when she makes her table arrangements. Therefore, all table appointments should be placed in convenient positions. Correct, functional place settings help make the act of eating a comfortable, pleasant experience.

The term "cover" is often used to describe an individual place setting at a dining table. A cover generally consists of the dinnerware, glassware or beverage ware, flatware, and linens to be used by each person. The amount of space required for each cover may vary in width, depending on the size of the table, but dining is more comfortable if at least 24 inches can be allowed for each cover.

If planning a seated dinner, follow this rule of thumb: Table covers are based on common sense, with the menu determining what items are needed for each cover. The order of courses indicates the placement of the glassware and flatware with the old saying, "start from the outside and work your way in," generally being true. This simply means that at each cover, the flatware for the first course is on the outside, farthest from the plate. As plates and flatware are used, they are cleared for successive courses, and the next utensil in line is used. This is done for convenience during dining and to give the cover a balanced appearance throughout the meal.

Obviously, the first step in setting the table is to lay the tablecloth, runner, or place mats. If using a traditional tablecloth, an overhang of about 12 inches will look best, and every effort should be made to remove any creases or wrinkles.

Place mats can be laid flush with the table edge or about 1 to 1½ inches from the edge. On a round or oval table, lay rectangular mats so that the corners are flush with the table edge (see Table Coverings, page 58).

The napkins can be folded and laid next, although you may prefer to do this last. At a formal dinner, the napkin should always be folded very simply and placed on the service plate. But for a formal luncheon or informal meal, the napkin is usually folded and laid to the left of the cover beside the fork or forks.

The menu determines what flatware is needed for each place setting; the order in which the courses are to be eaten indicates the placement of the flatware.

A creative hostess may have unique ideas for napkin presentation (see napkin folding examples, pages 60 to 63). Some hostesses may like to see the napkin softly "spilling" from the bowl of the wine glass while others admire napkins that gently drape or hang over the edge of the table. But in its most traditional position, the napkin should be folded in a long, narrow rectangle and placed entirely on the place mat so that the edge closest to the table lines up with the handle ends of the flatware and the outside rim of the plate.

The napkin should traditionally be folded so that the open corner of the napkin is in the lower right or lower left corner; this allows the napkin to be picked up and opened with a gentle shake of the left hand while the right hand smooths it across the lap. Napkins do vary in size—the 12-inch napkin is customarily used for breakfast and lunch. The 18-inch or larger napkin is reserved for dinner.

Always aim to keep the amount of flatware used to a minimum (see Flatware and Holloware, page 67); flatware that is placed on a cover and not used is intimidating and confusing. Generally, there should be no more than three pieces of flatware on each side of the plate. Knives and spoons go to the right of the plate, with each knife's cutting edge facing the plate. Bouillon or soup spoons go to the extreme right; if seafood or cocktail forks are used, they go to the right of the soup spoon. All other forks should go to the left of the plate and should be lined up in this order, from the outside in: salad fork, fish fork, and meat or dinner fork.

Laying the flatware for dessert is no problem unless a fork is to be used. When a fork is needed to eat dessert, it must be laid so that there is no doubt as to its intended use. If a menu does not include a salad, the dessert fork can be laid to the right of the dinner fork. When the menu does include a salad, lay the fork you intend for dessert above the dinner plate, allowing the tines to point to the right. When this is done, it is unlikely that anyone will use the dessert fork for salad because it is not in the expected position. When a special beverage, such as coffee, is served with the dessert only, lay the beverage spoon above the fork with the bowl pointing to the left.

If the table is completely cleared before dessert, the dessert flatware can be laid just before dessert is served. In this case, the dessert fork and spoon can be laid to the right of each cover. Another alternative is to place the dessert fork on the dessert plate along with the food and the beverage spoon on the coffee saucer with the handle of the spoon parallel to the handle of the coffee cup.

Traditionally, all regular dinner flatware should be laid so that the handle ends line up with the outer rim of the plate. If a place mat is used and it is placed away from the edge of the table, the flatware is laid so that handle ends are aligned with the edge of the place mat. Large serving pieces of flatware that are placed on the table should usually be placed to the right of the serving dish or platter.

You may prefer to place beverage glasses after they have been filled to avoid an accident while pouring at the table. In this case, the glasses are placed on a tray, filled, carried to the table, and placed. On the other hand, if water glasses are filled at the table, a pitcher should be used. The chilled water can be poured before guests sit down and replenished throughout the meal.

Glassware is positioned above the knife in order of use, with the water glass nearest the knife tip. The dessert wine glass should be closest to the table edge.

Wines are generally not poured until all guests are seated and the appropriate course is presented. The wine should be served first to the host; he checks the flavor before he or a servant serves the rest of the guests. To prevent wine from spilling when pouring from a bottle, turn the neck of the bottle gently as you lift the bottle mouth away from the glass. The bottle can also be wiped with a clean napkin between servings.

Water glasses should be placed at the tip of the knife. Additional glasses are positioned in order of use and placed successively closer to the table edge. Ideally, only three or four glasses should ever appear on a cover at the same time. The water glass should be placed first, the sherry glass (for soup course) or white wine glass second, the red wine or champagne glass third, with the dessert wine glass being last and easiest to reach. Each glass should be removed when the course it accompanied is completed, with the exception of the dessert wine glass which remains on the table. Water or iced tea may be served with the entire meal; if so, that glass would remain on the table.

Service plates, when used, are in front of guests when they are seated. If warmed dinner plates are to be used, they will be brought in when the entrée is served.

Bread and butter plates should be placed to the left of the cover near the tip of the fork. Unless the salad is served as a separate course, the salad plate can be placed in several different positions. If no bread and butter plate is included in the cover, place the salad plate at the tip of the fork. But if both bread and butter plates and salad plates are included, place the salad plate to the left and a little below the bread and butter plate.

Accessory items for the table might include salt and pepper containers, containers for butter and condiments, and, when absolutely necessary, ashtrays. For an informal dinner, a salt and pepper container for every two or three guests is correct. A wide variety of containers and small open dishes may be used. On a formal table, silver or silver and crystal salt and pepper containers are placed directly above the plates, with at least one set for two guests. Containers of condiments are not set on a formal table but are passed on the server's tray, if needed.

On a truly formal table, there should be no ashtrays during the meal. Nowadays, most hostesses prefer that guests not smoke during a dinner party; the prudent guest will always ask the hostess her preference before lighting a cigarette or cigar.

Example of a formally arranged seated table setting:

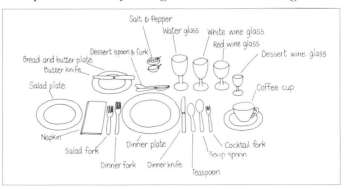

Creating a Style

Let floral arrangements echo the style and mood you wish to create throughout your home. There is something very appealing and inviting to guests when there is a visual expression of personality.

31

When having an informal dinner party, try serving the different menu courses in different areas of your home. You'll find the terrace is a delightful spot for appetizers or dessert.

Setting the Mood

Your personal style is never more apparent than on those occasions when you entertain guests. The decisions you make about the location for the party or dinner, the decorations and flowers, the table appointments, and the entertainment will set the stage and create a mood that reflects your taste and style.

There was a time when large palatial ballrooms were common, but today's homes tend to have smaller rooms. Even so, we've all been to parties where an inventive thinker has taken advantage of a small space and created a charming, intimate setting.

Magical settings are not all that difficult to achieve. First of all, never limit yourself to entertaining just in the dining room. Consider the charm your kitchen or den has to offer.

When you have a large party, you can spread out into the hallways, the library, the playroom, or even the garage. Don't forget the possibility of entertaining your guests on the deck or patio. And poolside parties are always beautiful and refreshing. Another summertime idea is to place blankets and bales of hay outside under the trees or in the garden to make a comfortable dining spot. Sometimes you may even be able to use your garage, driveway, or parking area to set up eating or dancing space.

Doing the unexpected can be intriguing—a closet can be turned into a bar, and a piano or end table can double as a serving area. Look for attractive architectural features and focus on them. Serve beverages from an open space under a staircase, or set up a buffet in front of pretty fan windows. You may even want to serve appetizers outside under a large shade tree, the main course on the porch, and end with dessert indoors in the den or kitchen.

To find the best areas for at-home entertaining, walk through each room and around the outside of the house, and carefully consider each potential spot. Size up the situation honestly but imaginatively. Keep in mind that plants, balloons, flowers, special lighting, a glowing fireplace, and pretty table appointments can do wonders for an otherwise dull room. If you are not happy with the interior locations, then consider moving your dinner or party outdoors.

Once the location is chosen, turn your attention to the selection of the dining table. The table certainly does not have to be located in the dining room, but it should be positioned so that guests have plenty of room to slide their chairs back and forth. Although the top of the table can be covered with a cloth or mats, it should still be in fairly good shape. A bumpy or uneven surface can be made smooth by adding a felt pad.

Before you select your table, consider the number of people to be seated during dinner. Ideally, about 24 inches should be allotted per person, but at a very informal dinner you can squeeze guests in until they run out of knee space. Sometimes, depending on the occasion, the crowding can help create a more jovial spirit.

The shape of the dining table should also coordinate with the room in which it will be placed. Round tables look good in square rooms and oval tables work well in rectangular rooms. Rectangular tables are ideal for long, wide rooms. Many hostesses like round tables because all guests face each other; it is felt that the circular shape stimulates conversation, rather than forcing discussions to the right or left as a rectangular table tends to do.

This doesn't mean that you will need to go out and buy a round dining table. An inexpensive solution is to have 48-inch rounds cut from particle board. The rounds can be placed on top of card tables and draped with a cloth. When not in use, the rounds can be stored under a bed. Round surfaces that fold in half are also available through several mail-order sources. These, too, can be used on top of card tables and stored conveniently in a closet or under a bed.

If space is limited, remember that side chairs or armless dining chairs take up less room. Enameled or metal folding chairs can certainly be used. Plain metal folding chairs are not very pretty, but loose slipcovers can make them extremely attractive. If you entertain large crowds, it is probably easier to rent additional chairs. Of course, you could always go in with a friend and split the cost of a large set of extra chairs, storing half at each house. In fact, this is a good way to obtain the additional flatware, table linens, china, glassware, vases, and other items that are needed for entertaining.

The type of lighting you select can go a long way toward providing mood and atmosphere. Always use soft-light or pink-light bulbs for a more flattering glow. Bright, glaring overhead lights are a definite no. It is a good idea to add rheostats, or dimmer switches, to major lights, particularly the dining room fixture. Turn up all the lights when guests first arrive—this tends to stimulate conversation and add excitement. But once the party is going, you can dim the lights. Spot lighting is also very attractive, especially when focused on a pretty plant or painting.

Candles have always been a favorite lighting technique for hostesses. Tiny votive candles are wonderful for creating atmosphere. Try grouping them in windows, on the fireplace mantel, around floral arrangements, on top of mirrors, and certainly on the dining table. Purchase votive candles by the case so that you will always have plenty on hand. And be sure to select a brand that burns slowly—good ones will last through an entire evening.

Tapered candles are always nice on a fancy table, but avoid having them flicker at eye level. If tapers are used, it is proper to place at least four on a formal dining table. Sometimes the base of a tapered candle will not fit into the candle holder. If the end of the candle is too large, try trimming it with a warm knife or soften it under hot water. If the base is too small for the holder, a quick remedy is to wrap a small strip of plastic wrap around the end before wedging it into the holder.

Liquid or floating candles produce a nice effect on a dining table. You can fill a pretty crystal bowl with water, topping it with about ½-inch of vegetable oil. Then float clear plastic discs containing wicks on top; the discs can often be purchased from hardware stores, craft shops, or florists. For an impressive presentation, try floating floral blooms in the container along with the floating wicks.

A casual, festive effect for outdoor entertaining can be achieved with luminarias. To create these special lights, anchor small paper bags with sand and nestle a small votive or utility-type candle in the center. Line the bags up along your driveway, around the pool, or outline the deck or patio with them. Be sure not to use luminarias when it is windy or if the grass is dry.

Strings of tiny white lights or fairy lights can also be used to create a special mood. Place the lights outside on shrubs or inside on large plants. Ficus or fig trees, greenery garlands, and crepe myrtles look especially magical when covered with these tiny lights. Kerosene lanterns are also appropriate for casual parties. Place the lanterns around the deck or patio or inside in the kitchen or den in a safe, out-of-the-way spot.

Music is one mood-setting device that you just don't want to be without. Live music can turn any party into an event. The gentle liveliness of a string quartet or combo or the soothing sounds of a harpist will provide the perfect background for a relaxing meal. A pianist playing during cocktails or coffee will often cause the conversation to take off happily. The sound of a jazz saxophone or an exciting reggae band will get everyone in a festive, dancing mood.

Before hiring performers, ask friends if they have heard the musicians perform and can make suggestions. Always get references of potential performers; never hire the

entertainment sight unseen. If there isn't a talent agency in your area, call local music teachers, the nearest symphony office, restaurant club, or college and high school offices. Be sure the musicians understand what type of party you are planning, where they will be performing, who they will be playing for, the expected hours of performance, and the mood you are aiming for. It is a good idea to have the musicians visit the location in advance to check out the facilities. Discuss whether or not dancing is planned and what type of sound system will be used.

If you are having a small dinner party and prefer not to have live musicians, then consider using tapes of your favorite dinner music. Another alternative that can be fun for a casual party is to hire someone to spin records, or find out if you can rent a jukebox. And never hesitate to spontaneously play the piano or guitar at your own party—it's a guaranteed way to delight guests.

Large-Scale Entertaining

"The more the merrier" is certainly true if large-scale events are carefully thought out. For example, for a large crowd it is easier for the hostess if the food can be made in advance and is the type that can stand reheating or will still look good after standing an hour or two. Foods that require last-minute preparation are usually too demanding for large-scale preparation. It is also important that the food be easy for guests to handle while standing, since casual buffets are the typical way to serve a large crowd.

Lack of space can also be a problem when accommodating a large crowd, especially when entertaining at home. If you don't have one large, spacious room, then perhaps you can open up the entire house and let guests drift from room to room.

An alternative is to rent a tent. If the party is a big, important occasion, a large tent and several service tents can be rented. In this case, it is best to discuss your plans

A creative arrangement of candles and crystal sets the mood and provides a pretty focal point for a buffet.

in detail with the rental company and the caterer about the table placement, as well as the areas for food preparation and cleanup. If necessary, you can even rent a dance floor.

Always get the advice of a landscape architect or consult someone at the tent company about the best placement of a tent. Usually these experts will consider things that may not have occurred to you, such as the flow of fallen rainwater and access to electrical outlets. Be sure to arrange for the tents to be delivered and set up the day before the event. A good rental agency will guarantee prompt delivery and pickup.

There are all sorts of attractive tents available. You probably should select the color of the tent based on the color of the tablecloths, napkins, and decorations that will be used. And don't forget to request plastic side shields in case of rain and fans or heaters in case of extreme hot or cold weather.

A banquet hall or club room can make a wonderful place to host guests graciously. By adding your own decorations, flowers, and entertainment, the room can be made to represent your style and personality. If the room is too large, divide it up by arranging the tables in a decorative fashion, and partition unused corners with folding screens. Large floral arrangements, ice sculptures, tall trees, centerpieces, and spot lighting can also add interest and character. By lighting areas of the room you want to emphasize and leaving the unused areas dimly lighted, you can draw the guests toward spots of interest.

A rented tent is an attractive, affordable way to add space for entertaining. Some small tents are so easy to assemble that you may want to do it yourself.

Luminarias provide beautiful mood lighting that is quite dramatic when used to outline walkways or pools.

consider outlining the area with citronella candles or bug-repellent torches. Take plenty of blankets, chairs, or bales of hay to stretch out on, and plan ahead for toilet facilities.

An outdoor swimming pool can make a beautiful setting for a dinner party. The pool will look lovely filled with a blanket of balloons or floating floral blooms. At night, you could outline the pool with tiny votive candles, luminarias, or plants decked with fairy lights. Some hostesses take a humorous approach and fill empty pools with plastic floating rafts topped with inflatable toys and cartoon characters.

Anytime you use tablecloths outdoors, be sure to anchor them with clips or staples. If it is windy, don't use candles, as they may catch the centerpiece or the cloth on fire.

Outdoor Entertaining

It is no wonder that Southerners have always liked to entertain outdoors. Some of our spectacular gardens and rolling hillsides make breathtaking backdrops for social gatherings. Just imagine loading guests onto a wagon filled with hay and heading for the closest meadow, or rounding up a group of agreeable horses for guests to go on a trail ride and picnic. Better yet, load guests into a van, and treat them to a box lunch while en route to your favorite swimming hole or football game.

These events can and should be relaxing and fun, but always make a trial run the week before to be sure you have thought of everything. Try to clear outdoor locations of ant beds, and spray in advance for bugs and mosquitoes;

The weather is the main variable to be concerned about when entertaining outdoors, but in most cases, it can be dealt with. Bright sunlight can be shaded with a tent; dark-colored tablecloths, napkins, and plates decrease reflections. High temperatures are uncomfortable, but if you are using a tent, air conditioning can be pumped in and circulated with the help of large fans. In the summer, be particularly careful not to leave food out for long periods of time; anything with meat or dairy products will spoil quickly.

Cold weather can also present a problem. On very cold days a tent will need to be heated with heaters. If the party is casual and it is safe to do so, you may want to light several bonfires. On days when the temperature dips, put out plenty of hot coffee and cocoa, and make sure the food is hot and hearty.

Cover your table with a pretty cloth and fill old pitchers with bouquets of wildflowers for a simple, feminine setting.

As our lifestyles have become more casual and relaxed, so have our floral arrangements. Many of today's hostesses, no matter how busy they are, seem to enjoy taking the time to create their own unique floral arrangements. Sometimes the creations are quite simple and sometimes they are very dramatic.

Sparse arrangements, often single blooms, displayed in any number of unlikely containers are now fashionable. For example, a single, interestingly shaped tulip or a perfectly formed rosebud placed in an unusual vase and lighted with a spotlight can fill an entire room with color and drama. Antique milk pitchers can be filled with wildflowers and Queen Anne's lace for a pretty country table. Or fill your grandmother's silver urn with pastel roses for a romantic bouquet. The combinations are unlimited.

When entertaining, flowers can brighten any area of your home—the kitchen, powder room, even the hallway. But floral presentation is most important on the dining table. Make

Festive Floral Arrangements

Whether used in massive arrangements or as a single bloom, flowers add color, luster, and glamour to tabletops and rooms. There was a time when floral arrangements came from a professional florist; upon delivery, they were placed in the center of the dining table, where they reigned in a tightly formed design that looked artificial.

sure that whatever blooms you select for the dining area have little or no perfume, as this could interfere with the taste and aroma of the food. Also, it is important that flowers on a dining table not hinder conversation or hide the guests. One way to prevent these problems is to create very tall, airy arrangements that are perhaps three- to four-feet high. This effect is very impressive, leading guests to feel as though they are dining underneath the centerpiece.

A simple and charming dining table floral arrangement is created by using several small bud vases, each containing a single bloom. You can use the same or different types of flower. When the vases are placed on a mirrored table runner, the effect is that of a crystal garden in full bloom.

Still another creative centerpiece can be formed by clustering a collection of favorite objects—tiny baskets, boxes, or antique toys—down the center of the table or one or two in front of each guest's place. Then tuck flowers, held securely in water-filled vials, into the grouping. Cover the vials with moss or leaves.

Fruits, vegetables, and flowers can also be combined for an attractive arrangement. A cantaloupe, honeydew, or spaghetti squash can be carved and formed into a vase to hold orchids or lilies. Or create a natural container for roses by carving out a dark, shiny eggplant or by coring an apple. Just cut a thin slice from the bottom to steady the fruit or vegetable, and insert tiny water-filled vials of flowers.

Vegetables and fruits such as artichokes, cabbages, pineapples, pumpkins, squash, apples, and pears can be combined for a striking table arrangement. Fill in empty spaces with pecans, walnuts, lemons, limes, and grapes. Violets, geraniums, begonias, chrysanthemums, dogwood blossoms, marigolds, or almost any other flower can be added to round out a handsome display.

Anyone who undertakes making her own floral creations will want to gradually collect an ample supply of vases and baskets. Almost anything that will hold water can be used as a vase. And if it won't hold water, you can insert a simple plastic or glass container as a liner.

A supply of bud vases is invaluable, as these can be grouped together or used separately throughout the house. A large round bubble or fishbowl-type vase is ideal for bouquets of sturdy-stemmed roses, daffodils, gladiolus, or tulips. Cylinder vases work nicely with arrangements that don't contain many flowers. Very large containers with wide

It is possible to build stunning arrangements that consist primarily of fruits and vegetables. The trick is to combine them in a soft, flowing fashion. Delicate flowers or greenery can be used to fill in where needed.

mouths are a better choice for heavier bouquets that may include branches from fruit trees, dogwoods, or magnolias.

Baskets are also a versatile container to use when entertaining. They can hold plants, flatware, napkins, flowers, or food. Line the baskets with a variety of fabrics, tie them with ribbons, or spray them to match your color scheme. If putting food or flowers in them, line them with plastic wrap or plastic bags and aluminum foil. This will protect the baskets and your table surface from accidental leakage.

Balloons can be used with flowers to add height to an arrangement and to create a whimsical look. If you want the balloons to stay afloat, they can be filled with helium. Long, bright-colored streamers can be used to tie balloons to chandeliers or to the backs of chairs. A delightful effect can be created when the entire ceiling of a room is covered with solid-colored, helium-filled balloons, with the streamers floating down to touch the heads of guests.

There are many professional florists available to help you create whatever decorative look you desire. But, if you have a limited budget, you may want to find a way to buy directly from a floral wholesaler and do the arrangements yourself. Of course, the easiest and most exciting source of flowers can be your own yard or garden. If you don't grow flowers yourself, ask neighbors and friends if they are willing to share what is growing in their yards. And always keep an eye out for what is growing in the open fields of nearby rural areas.

When creating floral arrangements yourself there are some tricks of the trade to bear in mind. For starters, you obviously will want to use flowers that are as fresh as possible. Therefore, you should cut flowers in the morning when their water content is highest, not on a hot, sunny afternoon. Some people prefer to cut flowers at night, leaving them to soak up water overnight. If purchasing the flowers, look for crisp, bright stems; the blooms should not be droopy and the petals should have no dark edges. Don't select buds that are tightly closed; they often never open completely—the exceptions to this rule are gladiolus, lilies, and tulips.

As you pick the flowers, remove all the bottom leaves, especially any that will be under the water line. Put the cut flowers in deep, lukewarm water as soon as possible. If

Fresh flowers are a precious investment; you will want to condition each stem so that the flowers will look fresh for as long as possible.

this isn't possible, wrap them loosely in damp newspaper, or sprinkle them with water, seal them in a plastic bag, and store the bag in a cool, shady spot. After placing in water, leave the flowers to soak for up to 12 hours. This gives the flowers a chance to drink in a new supply of water and revive themselves after being cut.

On most flowers, the stems should be cut on the diagonal to "condition" or increase the surface area for the intake of water. In fact, some florists prefer to do their diagonal trimming while holding the stems under water. The stems of woody plants—lilac, quince, dogwood, apple, or hydrangea, should be bruised with a wooden mallet or hammer; then about three inches of the bark should be scraped off from the stem end. An alternative to this method is to cut the woody stem end into a series of upward slits with a sharp knife. Sometimes, simply breaking woody stems, rather than cutting, can give the same effect of allowing for better water intake.

Some flowers, including poinsettias, poppies, and daffodils, produce a milky sap which clouds the water and hinders moisture absorption. These varieties will benefit from placing the stems in a bucket of boiling water for about a minute, then placing in cold water and leaving for several hours. Another method that can be used, but may be more difficult, is to singe the cut stems with a flame until they blacken; then place in cool water.

There are many different "recipes" that have been tried through the years to help give cut flowers a longer life. Many people use aspirin or a combination of aspirin and a teaspoon of sugar. The aspirin keeps the water clear, and the sugar feeds the flowers. Charcoal, alum, or bleach can also be added to help keep the water clear. The most popular recommendation is to soak the cut flowers in plain, lukewarm water; then add one teaspoon of bleach per quart of water to be added to the vases. Another solution is to add a commercial floral freshener to the vase water.

Even before you go about the business of selecting your flowers, think ahead to the tools that will be needed to complete your arrangements. The following items could be assembled and stored in a large, handy basket; while they all aren't absolutely necessary, they will help you create more beautiful, longer-lasting arrangements:

1. One or more large buckets to hold the flowers for soaking.
2. At least two knives: A large one for cutting thick, woody stems and a small one for cutting other stems on an angle.
3. A hammer and a cutting board to use for conditioning woody stems.
4. A pair of sharp clippers.
5. A rose thorn stripper.
6. An ample supply of oasis or foam for holding flowers.

7. A variety of different-sized frogs to anchor arrangements.
8. A supply of florist's tape to secure the oasis in containers and to cover wires or tie flowers together.
9. A product called "stickum" to anchor oasis or frogs in containers.
10. Floral wire for strengthening flower stems.
11. Water vials to give individual blooms their own source of water.
12. A small bottle of bleach or commercial flower freshener to keep the water clear and to prolong the life of the blooms.
13. A small bottle of ammonia for cleaning out vases.
14. A spray bottle to keep arrangements moist and fresh.

Proceed slowly and carefully in planning how to best display your flowers. Always try to plan each arrangement to fit the desired location. Consider the design, the appropriate size or scale, balance, and harmony before starting the display. After conditioning the flowers, it is a good idea to hold them loosely bunched against the container you have chosen and assess the combination. Once you are happy with the coupling of the flowers and the container, check the ensemble to see if it works well against your chosen background. If so, you are ready to build your creation. Consider heights carefully, keeping in mind an imaginary outline as you place the basic outline foliage. Move the stems around freely within this imaginary outline to obtain the desired effect; stop and stand back often to observe. Once you have created the basic outline shape with the greenery or foliage, fill in with additional color by adding stems of flowers.

Knowing when to stop adding stems is very important. Never continue to add flowers until your arrangement looks contrived. Remember that the brightest colors make the boldest statements, and that irregularity can add interest and charm to the arrangement. Take time to experiment; consider the effect you are aiming for, and most important, respect the natural line and form of the flowers.

Fine Touches

A gracious hostess is eager to bring out all her finest treasures to share with guests. The enjoyment of fine art, beautiful flowers, crystal, and silver will lead to a memorable evening.

Serving Liquor, Punch, and Coffee

The gracious hostess will offer guests something to drink upon their arrival—iced tea, coffee, soft drink, wine, or spirited beverage. However, an elaborate, prominently displayed bar is not necessary for a small dinner party. In fact, a large bar may tend to downplay the importance of the dinner.

For a small dinner party, you may want to offer a limited selection of beverages, perhaps wine or champagne, fruit juice, and maybe one special mixed drink. If you do offer one special cocktail, you may want to think of it as an additional appetizer on your menu. For example, if piña coladas are served upon arrival, then they could take the place of an appetizer on the menu.

For a large party, you will want to offer a wider variety of mixed drinks. If working with a caterer or bartender, ask his help in estimating how much liquor you will need. Consider whether the guests are heavy drinkers or teetotalers, and adjust your order accordingly.

The amount of liquor you should plan on per person depends on several factors—the type of party, how long the party will last, and the type of food to be served. To help in planning, you can estimate that there are four 6-ounce servings in each 750-milliliter bottle of wine. There are about 17 drinks per 750-milliliter bottle of liquor when 1½ ounces are used per drink. Plan on approximately two drinks per hour per guest. One 10-ounce bottle of mixer per person is usually sufficient.

One case of champagne will serve about 50 people; you should be able to get four to six glasses per bottle, depending on the size of your glasses. For large casual parties, a keg of beer is perfectly acceptable and makes for easy serving. A keg will adequately serve 30 to 40 guests. If punch is served at a party or reception, a gallon will serve about 24 people.

Always insist that liquor be measured with a jigger, using 1½ ounces of 80-proof liquor per drink. Try to pace guests at one to two drinks per hour. Cheese, vegetables, meats, and oily appetizers, such as bacon-wrapped water chestnuts or fried mushrooms, will usually slow the consumption of alcohol. On the other hand, salty snacks, such as peanuts,

If you entertain frequently and have a home bar, be sure to do an inventory on a regular basis, checking to see that an adequate supply of liquor and bar equipment is on hand.

will encourage guests to drink more. Some caterers believe that less alcohol is consumed when there is a one-to-one ratio of males to females and when the background music has a fast, lively beat.

There are a number of ways to make the bar area look inviting. For small gatherings, set beverage supplies on an attractive cart, tray, table, or counter, and let the host or one of the guests serve as the bartender. For larger parties, a more formal, organized bar and a professional bartender will be needed.

Service bars for large events can be located near the center of the party area but are more convenient if set up in uncongested areas. When space is a consideration, you might try turning an unused closet or pantry into a bar. Otherwise, cover a six- to eight-foot table with a cloth, place a colorful waterproof drape over it, and let this serve as the base for your bar.

Check your supply of bar equipment before each party. For each bar you should have on hand a couple of large pitchers, an ice bucket, several jigger measures, a long spoon or stirrer, several corkscrews, a citrus zester, and a small sharp knife and cutting board for slicing lemons, limes, oranges, olives, and onions. A trash can, cocktail napkins, and ice scoop or tongs are also necessary. You will need to have two to three napkins per person for a three-hour party. As for ice, commercially purchased ice is usually clear and odorless and makes for a fresher tasting drink than ice from a home freezer that may have picked up food odors. Plan on purchasing about ¾ to 1 pound of crushed ice per guest.

Opinions are mixed as to what should be kept on hand in a home bar. There was a time when a good supply of vodka, Scotch, bourbon, and gin would have been sufficient. But contemporary drinkers often prefer wine, beer, and liqueurs, so these should also be added to the list.

If you entertain on a regular basis and you want to build a current, well-stocked home bar, always try to have the following on hand:

THE WELL-STOCKED BAR

LIQUOR

Vodka - 2 (750-milliliter) bottles
Scotch - 2 (750-milliliter) bottles
Light rum - 1 (750-milliliter) bottle
Dark rum - 1 (750-milliliter) bottle
Gin - 2 (750-milliliter) bottles
Bourbon - 2 (750-milliliter) bottles
Blended whiskey - 2 (750-milliliter) bottles

LIQUEUR

Amaretto (almond-flavored) - 1 (750-milliliter) bottle
Benedictine (cognac-based) - 1 (750-milliliter) bottle
Cointreau, Grand Marnier, or Triple Sec
    (orange-flavored) - 1 (750-milliliter) bottle
Crème de Menthe (mint-flavored) - 1 (750-milliliter)
    bottle
Kahlúa (coffee-flavored) - 1 (750-milliliter) bottle

WINE

White wine - 4 (750-milliliter) bottles
Red wine - 4 (750-milliliter) bottles
Rosé wine - 2 (750-milliliter) bottles
Sherry - 2 (750-milliliter) bottles
Dry vermouth - 1 (750-milliliter) bottle
Sweet vermouth - 1 (750-milliliter) bottle
Sparkling wine or champagne - 2 (750-milliliter) bottles

BEER

Light beer - 2 six-packs   Dark beer - 1 six-pack
Imported beer - 2 six-packs

MIXERS

Sparkling water   Ginger ale   Tomato juice
Club soda   Soft drinks   Orange juice
Tonic water

Here is an attractive, economical way to ice down beverages—just line your favorite large basket with plastic bags and aluminum foil before filling with ice. Then decorate the basket with flowers.

A large acrylic or lucite tub provides an attractive way to chill bottles of wine. When placed in the entryway, guests can be greeted with a glass of wine.

Of course, if you are planning for a special guest or for a large crowd, you will need to tailor your liquor stock to meet those needs. If serving a large party, you may consider purchasing large quantities of liquor from a wholesaler or broker; he will be able to sell to you by the full or mixed case. If you need to chill a large quantity of wine, beer, or soft drinks, do so in ice chests, new trash cans, or tin tubs filled with ice. Some hostesses who routinely use such containers for icing down large quantities of beverages have gone so far as to paint the containers with decorative designs. You can arrange the containers outside your kitchen near the back door, or place them out of sight beneath a cloth-draped bar.

Another attractive way to chill beverages is to fill unused punch bowls or large flower pots with ice; then place soft drinks or wine carafes down in the ice. Even a large basket can be used to hold ice if lined first with plastic and then aluminum foil.

A champagne fountain can be rented to serve a large number of guests efficiently with any clear punch or champagne. A fountain will operate with as little as three bottles of champagne or as much as five gallons of punch. The beverage should be chilled thoroughly before adding it to the fountain, but you can add small chunks of ice or a few ice cubes to the bowl of the fountain to help keep the beverage cold.

You will probably want to offer coffee to guests at most functions. The easiest way to do this is with the help of a large coffee maker. If you are unfamiliar with the operation of a large coffee maker, simply fill it to the desired level with cold water; add the ground coffee to the basket, cover with the top, and plug it in. When the coffee has finished brewing, remove the basket; the coffee will stay hot. However, you must plan ahead when using a large coffee maker because it takes approximately a half hour to brew coffee in 30-cup coffee makers and an hour or more in 60- to 100-cup coffee makers. When purchasing coffee, remember that one pound of beans provides about 4¾ cups of ground coffee, which will make about 75 cups of brewed coffee. Use the following to estimate amounts:

for 30 cups of coffee, use about 2 cups of ground coffee
for 60 cups of coffee, use about 4 cups of ground coffee
for 100 cups of coffee, use about 6¼ cups of ground coffee

There are so many delightful flavors of coffee available today that you may want to sample several of them before deciding on one to serve your guests. Some hostesses take such pride in their coffee that it often becomes their hallmark; they make a point of always serving a particular type or flavor.

Selecting and Serving Wines

Serving wine with food should be a simple, pleasurable experience. The decision as to which wine to serve should not be taken too seriously, nor should it be made too hastily. A good hostess will never allow herself to become so overwhelmed with the vast number of wine choices that she researches and analyzes each selection to the point of allowing it to become a burden. On the other hand, a competent hostess should not fall into the trap of planning meals without giving any more thought to the wine than a quick reference to the "white wine with white meat, red wine with red meat" concept. A better rule of thumb to follow would be to serve a robust wine with a hearty main dish, and a lighter wine with a more delicate menu.

The best wine and food matches are usually achieved when a happy, middle-of-the-road attitude is taken toward selecting the wine. The fact is, any pleasant-tasting wine will taste good with food. However, there are occasions when lovers of food and wine take pleasure in seeing how close they can come to finding the perfect wine for their favorite recipe. And there is no doubt that, if you have the time and desire, you can discover some wonderful, harmonious food and wine matches.

There are several different approaches that can be taken when pairing wines with food. First, recognize that the concept of white wine with white meat and red wine with red meat is rather limiting and fails to take into consideration some of the other key elements that should influence your selection. Always keep these specific points in mind:

1. What is the main ingredient in the recipe?
2. Does the dish include a sauce? If so, what is the base or flavor of the sauce?
3. Are there any other flavoring agents? For example, is the dish salty or highly seasoned with herbs?
4. How was the dish prepared? Was it sautéed in butter or grilled, smoked, or simmered for hours?
5. Will the food be served hot or cold?
6. What kind of wines are available to you, and what price range fits your budget?

For example, if selecting a wine for Cornish hens, consider whether they are to be baked and basted with butter, rubbed with salt, coated with herbs, served with a sauce, or charred on the grill. Any of these procedures could dramatically alter the taste of the hens and thereby influence your wine selection.

As you consider each of these elements, let your thoughts progress to the point where you base your final selection on one of the following concepts—sameness, contrast, or intensity.

If you are selecting a wine based on the concept of sameness, simply pair wines with foods that seem to have the same or similar characteristics. For example, match a rich lobster dish with a richly flavored white Burgundy, a lightly sauced chicken dish with a light Chardonnay, an earthy beef and mushroom dish with an aged, earthy red wine, or a sweet dessert with a sweet Sauterne. The problem with the sameness concept is that it can become boring; the wine and food may taste too much alike. In other words, too much of a good thing can be hard to take.

The second concept—contrast—can be responsible for many exciting wine and food matches. A salty cheese served with a sweet wine can make a fabulous combination. Or try a crisp, dry white or dry red wine with fish. The acidity will serve the same purpose as a squeeze of lemon juice and will cut any strong taste.

But contrast must be practiced with caution. Sometimes the food and wine will contrast so much that the tastes fight each other and a pleasant match is impossible. The key to using the sameness and contrast concepts is to plan and anticipate in your mind which matches will be more harmonious. It is obviously to your advantage to have a good idea of the true flavor of the food from having prepared and eaten it in the past. It is also best to make your wine selections from wines you have sampled before; otherwise, you may prefer to seek the advice of a more experienced taster.

The third concept is intensity. Basically this concept revolves around the idea that simple wines require simply flavored foods and assertive wines can support highly spiced foods. This makes sense because a wine that has a strong, bold flavor can overwhelm a mild dish so that the food would seem to have no flavor at all. The opposite could occur if you paired a delicate wine with a robust dish. For example, the idea behind this concept would be to serve a bold wine with a spicy Indian or Szechwan dish or a mild wine with a delicately sauced French dish. When practicing the intensity concept, realize that selecting a bold wine for a bold dish does not guarantee a harmonious, tasty match. So, exercise care and make sure that the wine and food pairing is based on more than just intensity.

In summary, the concepts of sameness, contrast, and intensity will not automatically lead you to the perfect wine and food match. The concepts should be used as only part of the process of selection. However, they do provide a place to start the selection process. The ultimate selection will have to be made based on a combination of factors, and

Wines reveal their best qualities when served correctly; the bottle should be chilled to the correct temperature, the cork should be extracted properly, and the liquid should be poured into an appropriately shaped glass.

you will have to determine what makes the best match for each individual food and wine.

It can also make a difference if you are selecting wine or wines for an entire menu rather than for just a single dish. Keep in mind that the success of any match within a menu will be influenced by the preceding course and the wine that was served with it.

The best approach to take when planning wines for an entire menu is to begin by analyzing the wines for sweetness. Plan to serve your driest wines first and progress to the sweeter wines. Also, consider the color of the wines. You should serve white wines before light red wines, and

To open a bottle of chilled champagne or sparkling wine properly, tilt the bottle and point the cork away from guests and breakable objects. Then turn the bottle slowly in one direction while pulling out the cork.

And the opposite case occurs in winter; the taste for red wines seems to thrive on cold, wintry days.

The wine you select will reveal its best qualities when it is served correctly. For example, the bottle must be chilled to the right temperature, the cork should be extracted properly, and the wine should be served in an appropriately shaped glass.

Wine should be opened gently, using an opener that will enable you to extract the cork cleanly and smoothly. Most young red, white, and rosé wines are very simple to open. But you must take more care when removing the cork of an older red wine in order to avoid disturbing the sediment in the bottle. Champagnes and sparkling wines must also be opened gently to prevent the cork from flying off and to keep the wine from bubbling over.

Whatever its cost or design, a wine opener should have an evenly coiled, smooth screw that will enter the cork without causing it to break or crumble. A two-pronged extractor is a little more difficult for most people to use, but it does remove the cork without actually piercing it, which is helpful if you wish to reuse the cork.

To open most young red or white wines, stand the bottle upright and cut around the foil just below the protruding part of the bottle top, and remove the foil so that it will not touch the wine as it is poured. Then insert the screw of the opener into the center of the cork, twisting slowly. When the screw is firmly embedded, gently pull out the cork. Be sure to wipe off the rim of the bottle before serving or decanting the wine. If served directly from the bottle, twist the bottle gently as you pour to prevent dripping.

When opening an older red wine that contains sediment, first place it upright for a day or two before serving to allow the sediment to settle to the bottom; move the bottle as little as possible while uncorking. If the bottle hasn't been allowed to stand upright, serve it from a wine cradle so that you won't disturb the sediment as it is poured.

Champagne and sparkling wines are less likely to explode and bubble over upon opening if well chilled. But even if the champagne is cold, it must be opened with caution. Start by peeling back the foil wrapper and exposing the wire cage or muzzle. Unwind the wire with one hand while holding the cork down with the other hand; then remove

light red wines before dark red wines. Another way to look at the progression would be to serve the younger wines first and the older wines last.

Specific situations could force changes in these menu serving ideas, but for the most part, the guidelines are logical and practical. An exception is sweet wines, particularly Sauterne which is traditionally served as an appetizer wine or a dessert wine. Some floral champagnes may also work well when served with dessert. Another exception could also be discovered when the season or time of year comes into play. Heavy red wines tend not to be as pleasant served in the heat of summer as are lighter white wines.

the wire. Still holding the cork, angle the bottom of the bottle toward your chest and the neck away from guests or breakable objects. Grasp the cork with one hand and twist the bottle gently with the other hand. As added insurance, place a napkin over the cork.

There is always a question of when to decant, which means pouring the wine from the original bottle to another container before serving. There are several reasons for decanting wine: if an older wine contains sediment, if you wish to improve the bouquet and soften the taste of a young red wine, or if there are broken pieces of cork floating in the wine.

If you do decant wine, it is probably best to do so near serving time. If it is a young red wine, pour it into the decanter rapidly so that the wine will splash up the sides of the decanter and incorporate more air. If it is an older wine with heavy sediment and the cork has begun to crumble, place a funnel in the neck of the decanter and line it with cheesecloth or muslin and slowly pour through the funnel, stopping as soon as the sediment begins to appear. An older red wine may also be decanted by placing a flashlight or candle beneath the bottle as you start to pour to clearly see the sediment as it approaches the neck. As soon as you see the dark sediment, stop pouring immediately.

To taste fresh, wine should be at least a few degrees cooler than the temperature of the room in which it is to be served. A cooler temperature helps bring out the wine's flavor and bouquet. Since colder temperatures soften acidity, dry white and rosé wines should be chilled thoroughly before serving. Fresh, fruity red wines should be served at a cooler temperature than dry, tannic, older reds. Tannic, older red wines need a slightly warmer temperature to release their bouquet. The theory that red wines should be served at room temperature evolved because most dining rooms in times past were unheated. However, chill red wine briefly, because overchilling can exaggerate the tannin or astringent taste and slow the development of the bouquet. Champagne and sparkling wines should be chilled in an ice bucket and served in chilled glasses.

To swirl the wine, grasp the stem of the glass rather than the bowl in order not to raise the temperature of the wine. The ideal serving glass for most table wines should have a top rim that is narrower than the widest part of the bowl. Glasses used for red wine tend to be larger than those used for white or rosé wine to allow more room for swirling so that you can enjoy the bouquet and aroma.

Champagne or sparkling wines are best served in glasses that have long flute- or tulip-shaped bowls so that you can see the rising bubbles. Since the sparkling wine's bouquet is developed from the bursting bubbles rather than from swirling, the glasses can be filled almost to the top. Fortified wines like Sherry, Port, or Madeira are served in smaller, tulip-shaped glasses which are narrow at the rim.

Remember that wine is one of the most useful cooking condiments. One of the best white wines for cooking is dry white vermouth, which is a wine that has been flavored with herbs and spices. Wine can be used as a tenderizer and adds wonderful flavor to marinades. Red wine will add

Hold wine glasses by the stem rather than by the bowl. Large-bowled glasses are good choices for red wines and flute-shaped glasses are best for champagnes.

color as well as flavor to a dish, something you may want to avoid when cooking light-colored chicken or fish.

And a final note—store leftover wine or champagne by recorking the bottle and putting it in the refrigerator. This should extend its life an extra day or two.

Garnishing

Every hostess should strive to present guests with food that is as pleasing to the eye as it is to the palate. Garnishes give each plate of food a finished look and the cook an opportunity to be creative.

It is best to avoid garnishes that look complicated or contrived. Not only are they time-consuming and difficult to make, but often they look so whimsical that the plate takes on a silly appearance, thereby detracting from the importance of the food. The best garnishes are natural garnishes that can usually be found by looking at the list of ingredients in the recipe. For example, if the recipe calls for lemon juice, then lemon slices, lemon curls, or lemon zest would be appropriate natural garnishes.

Of course, a natural garnish cannot always be found within the recipe ingredient list. In that case, you might select a sprig of a fresh herb or berry fruit, or perhaps create a more elaborate garnish such as chocolate curls.

Today's grocery markets offer a wide selection of unusual garnishes. The small ornamental or miniature fruits and vegetables are perfectly suited for garnishing many dishes. And some markets sell edible floral blossoms; these offer one of the most striking ways to brighten a plate.

Edible floral garnishes have distinctive flavors—some are hot, some are sweet, some are herbal. When garnishing food with flowers, be careful to select edible varieties, for not all flowers are safe to eat. Some of the more common edible flowers include nasturtiums, rose petals, marigolds, violets, primroses, fruit tree blossoms, squash blossoms, and the flowers of many herbs—fennel, borage, and chives, to name a few. Never consume florist flowers; you don't know what pesticides may have been used. The best way to produce a glorious flower garnish is to grow your own from seed without any pesticides.

If you are a novice at creating garnishes, here are some hints to keep in mind.

Tips for choosing garnishes:

1. Use garnishes with the taste, color, and shape that complements the main ingredients in the dish. For example, gherkin pickles taste good with sandwiches, but not with fruit salad; tiny round onions may look monotonous with a platter of round meatballs.
2. Hot or cold garnishes can be served with hot foods, but only cold garnishes are best with cold foods.
3. Keep garnishes simple. Never spend more time on the garnish than you did preparing the food.
4. Judge the appropriateness of a garnish by how much it adds to the enjoyment of the food.

Tips for making garnishes:

1. Select fruit or vegetable garnishes by taste, size, proportion, color, and texture.
2. Hard vegetables, such as carrots and turnips, are easier to work with if they are at room temperature. To warm them in a hurry, place them in a pan of warm water for a few minutes before using.
3. Trim a thin slice from the bottom of a round fruit or vegetable to make it sit straight.
4. Soak garnishes made from leeks, green onions, and carrots in a bowl of ice water placed in the refrigerator until you are ready to use them. This will help them "set" or "curl."
5. Apples and pears turn brown when cut and exposed to air. To help keep their original color, rub or sprinkle with lemon juice as soon as they are cut.
6. Blanching carrots, broccoli, beans, and leeks will make them slightly tender and will heighten their natural color. To blanch vegetables, boil enough water to cover the vegetables. Place the vegetables in a wire basket or strainer; dip the basket into the boiling water for 5 to 15 seconds. Remove the basket and drain the vegetables. Rinse in cold water, then drain the vegetables again.

Chocolate garnishes are easy to make and ideal for garnishing most desserts. In most cases, the chocolate should first be melted. Unsweetened chocolate melts to a runny liquid, but when poured out onto a smooth surface, it hardens quickly into a solid form, thereby making it difficult to make chocolate curls. However, it is ideal for grating and for making chocolate shavings.

Semisweet chocolate retains its shape longer, making it easier to work with. This type of chocolate is ideal for making curls, ruffles, and cutouts. After it has been melted, this chocolate will set up into a more pliable stage before it solidifies. A sharp vegetable peeler can be used to form curls or ruffles (see page 54). A cookie cutter will make even, smooth cutouts. Melted semisweet chocolate is also ideal for piping abstract designs. Just fill a pastry bag fitted with a small tip and pipe a design onto wax paper. Once set, the designs can be placed on desserts.

Chocolate garnishes can be made in advance and stored in airtight containers in the refrigerator or freezer. Allow them to come to room temperature before taking them out of the containers or the chocolate will sweat, and the moisture will make it turn gray and lose its satiny sheen.

To melt chocolate, use a clean, dry saucepan. Even one drop of water in the saucepan can cause the chocolate to tighten and fail to melt. The key to melting chocolate is gentle heat; if melted at high temperatures, chocolate will scorch and stiffen. If melting 3 ounces (3 squares) or less, place chopped chocolate in a small, heavy saucepan over very low heat. If melting more than 3 ounces, place chopped chocolate in the top of a double boiler over simmering (not boiling) water. When chocolate is barely melted, remove from heat and stir with a wooden spoon until it is smooth. To melt 3 ounces of chopped chocolate in the microwave oven, place it in a glass measuring cup and microwave, uncovered, at MEDIUM (50% power) for 2 to 2½ minutes or until softened; then stir the chocolate until it is melted and smooth.

Try your hand at making the garnishes on the following pages. To make these garnishes, you will need the following: pastry decorating bag with tips, metal spatula, vegetable peeler, sharp paring knife, citrus zester, citrus stripper, soft pastry brush, and rolling pin.

Edible, pesticide-free flowers will spark dinner conversation. Their addition makes a plain green salad explode with color.

Chocolate abstract designs: Fill a pastry decorating bag fitted with a small tip with melted chocolate. Drizzle design on wax paper; freeze until firm. Let come to room temperature; gently lift off design.

Chocolate curls: Pour melted chocolate onto wax paper; spread into a 3-inch-wide strip. Let stand until cool, but not firm. Pull vegetable peeler across chocolate. Transfer curl to a paper plate. Chill.

Citrus zest or citrus strips: Holding fruit firmly in one hand, run citrus zester or citrus stripper firmly around the outer rind of the fruit to create continuous curls of desired length.

Citrus twists: Cut thin slices from lemons, limes, or oranges. With a paring knife, cut from the center of each slice outward through rind. Hold cut edges and gently twist in opposite directions.

Tomato rose: With a sharp paring knife, peel a paper-thin strip of peel, ¾-inch wide, from entire tomato. Coil strip tightly, fleshy side inward, gradually letting it become looser to form outer petals.

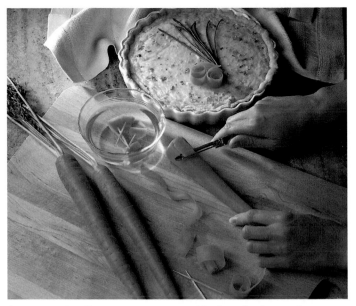

Carrot curls: Scrape carrot; cut thin lengthwise strips from carrot with a vegetable peeler. Roll strips up tightly; secure with wooden picks. Place in ice water; chill until set. Remove picks before garnishing.

Frosted berries or grapes: Beat an egg white until frothy. Paint berries or grapes with egg white, using a soft pastry brush. While wet, sprinkle with granulated sugar. Set aside to dry.

Apricot roses: Flatten dried apricot slices to ⅛-inch thickness. Shape one slice into a bud. Curl 5 to 7 slices around bud, pressing sticky side inward and curling top edges outward. Pinch at bottom.

Caring for Your Best

Pride and satisfaction are felt when you polish silver until it shines and gleams. Often passed down in families from mother to daughter, antique silver and holloware is typically ornate and valuable.

57

Table Coverings

Setting the table for guests is like setting the stage for a play. In the same way that the director seeks a backdrop that will allow for the best overall presentation, a hostess creatively combines linens, dinnerware, holloware, glassware, and flatware for a desired effect. It is with these table appointments that the hostess can ultimately create a picture of neatness, order, and beauty, or, unfortunately, one of chaos and confusion.

Gathering a wide and varied collection of table appointments can be an expensive undertaking. With this in mind, it makes sense for the beginning hostess to get her appointment collection off to a wise start. It is valuable to learn quickly what constitutes quality and which items have inherent charm. And, assuming that your linen, crystal, china, and silver are among your most prized possessions, you will want to know how to care for each of these items properly.

One of the easiest ways to change the look of a dining table is to change the linens. The term "linens" can be used broadly to include any type of fabric tablecloth, place mats, runners, or napkins. In most cases, linens should be selected to harmonize with the other table appointments, especially the dinnerware, as well as the dining area. Depending on the look you wish to create and the type of dinner you are planning, there is a variety of fibers, colors, textures, and designs to choose from.

When selecting tablecoverings, remember that heavily patterned dishes look best on plain or simple-patterned linens, and plain dishes or those with simple bands of color work better with patterned linens. However, there are exceptions to this; one of the most popular ways to combine patterned dishes with a patterned tablecloth is by using a solid service plate or charger under the dinner plate.

Another basic idea to keep in mind is that, in addition to being harmonious in color and design, linens should also be of a texture that is compatible with the other appointments. Textured fabrics and materials are generally more suitable for use with heavier looking dinnerware and glassware, while fine china and crystal tend to be more at home with sheer linens and lace.

If dressing a table for a formal dinner, it is up to you to determine how closely you want to follow the standard rules of etiquette. But a truly formal dinner requires a full-sized tablecloth that is large enough to allow for a 12- to 15-inch overhang on a square or rectangular table. Damask cloths for formal dinners can be white or pastel and usually have a woven design of the same color.

When a damask tablecloth is used, it is advisable, in most cases, to place it over a silence cloth or felt pad. Cloths with embroidery or lace can be placed directly over the bare table, but if you have a pretty lace cloth, you may want to place it over a solid-colored undercloth that will be decorative and will also protect the table.

The adventurous hostess who wishes to express the different aspects of her personality has the option of creating an endless collection of original table coverings. By varying combinations, the tone of your dinners can range from elegant to extremely casual. Quite often an idea for an unusual table covering can be discovered among items you have around the house—quilts, rugs, sheets, antique lace, embroidered items, pillow shams, paint drop cloths, scarves, bandannas, hand towels, and fabric right off the bolt, simply hemmed or cut with pinking shears to give the edges a zigzag finish.

To make your own rectangular or square tablecloth from a sheet or piece of fabric, measure the top surface width and length of the table; then add the drop length, plus hem, for each side.

A round tablecloth can be made by measuring the diameter of the table top plus twice the drop, plus twice the hem allowance. If the table is a very large round, it may be necessary to join two or three lengths of fabric to create the necessary width, especially if you want the cloth to reach the floor. Typically, a second width of fabric will need to be split and sewn onto the sides of the center piece to form a giant square. Then you will need to fold the fabric evenly into quarters. After determining half the diameter of the finished cloth, measure that distance on the fabric and draw a quarter circle; cut through all four layers along the marked line to make your round cloth. In a pinch, the width of a double-bed sheet or a king-size sheet can be used as a tablecloth. The ends can be puffed underneath

Look around your house for interesting objects to use as table coverings. Here, a fringed shawl is arranged over the table.

the table, or you can cut a round, floor-length cloth, using pinking shears to give the edge a zigzag finish. For a clean finish, fold under the hem allowance and machine stitch.

Napkins come in a variety of materials, ranging from damask to paper. Among the most popular fabrics used for napkins are linen or linen blends, cotton and cotton blends, and synthetic fibers. Each material is noted for its special qualities—linen for elegance, cotton for durability, synthetics for easy care, and paper for practicality.

Scarves, bandannas, kitchen or terry cloth towels, and dainty hand towels can serve as unique napkins and can even be take-home presents for your guests. For more formal entertaining, it is a good idea to have several dozen large square white damask or cotton napkins on hand. Today, most fabric napkins come in four sizes: 17-, 20-, 22-, and 24-inch square. Generally, the larger napkins are reserved for more formal use; smaller napkins are used for luncheons or informal dining.

The napkin is usually placed at the left of the cover beside the fork or forks. However, when covers are close together, the napkin may be placed in the center of the cover on the plate or service plate. The practice of placing the napkin to the left of the plate and placing the forks upon it is acceptable and practical only when dining outside, where it is necessary to anchor the napkin. This placement necessitates moving the forks in order to use the napkin and can therefore cause diners to drop their flatware. On occasions when place mats are used, the napkin may be placed on the mat, partly on the mat and partly on the table, or entirely on the table. Whatever position is used, lay the napkin so that its design and hem are lined up with the place mat.

Ideally, the napkin should be placed so that when it is picked up by one corner with the left hand, it will fall open, and the right hand can smooth it across the lap. Smaller, luncheon napkins should be open when in use. Larger, dinner-size napkins can be folded in half in the lap. Once the meal is finished and the guest is preparing to leave the table, the unfolded napkin should be placed to the left of the cover.

When a decorative touch is desired, napkins can be folded into interesting shapes. The following folds will work better if you start with clean, lightly starched, freshly pressed napkins. When creating a fold for the first time, practice with a paper napkin to avoid creasing your freshly laundered napkins. It is a good idea to fold napkins for a dinner party the day before the party. This will allow you to take your time and avoid last-minute frustrations.

These special folds will look prettier if used on solid-colored napkins or napkins where the design is woven into the fabric so that there will be no unfinished or unprinted side exposed.

BUFFET FOLD

A. Lay napkin open and flat. Fold the napkin in half to form a rectangle with folded edge at the bottom. Fold top edge of the first layer down 2 inches towards middle; then fold down again 2 inches towards bottom edge.

B. Turn napkin over. Bring right edge to center. Repeat, folding this section over on itself two more times in same direction.

C. Tuck flatware into pocket that is formed.

STRAW ROLL

A. Lay napkin open and flat with one corner pointing down towards you.

B. Starting at the bottom corner, roll napkin into a smooth tube.

C. Fold tube in half. Tie with long ribbons or tuck folded middle into a goblet or glass.

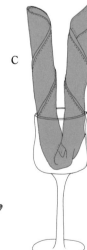

DIPLOMA ROLL

A. Lay napkin open and flat. Fold napkin in half to form a rectangle with folded edge at the top. Fold top right and bottom right corners in to meet and form a triangle.

B. Roll napkin all the way up from left to right.

C. Secure napkin with a ribbon or napkin ring.

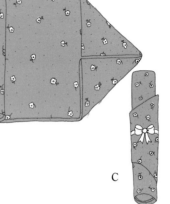

CUMMERBUND FOLD

A. Lay napkin open and flat. Fold napkin into quarters with closed corner pointing down towards you. Tightly roll top layer down to center.

B. Rotate napkin to the right so that roll runs on a diagonal from top left to bottom right.

C. Holding roll in the same position, fold left and right edges under until they meet and overlap slightly. The remaining rectangle should feature a band that runs diagonally from left to right.

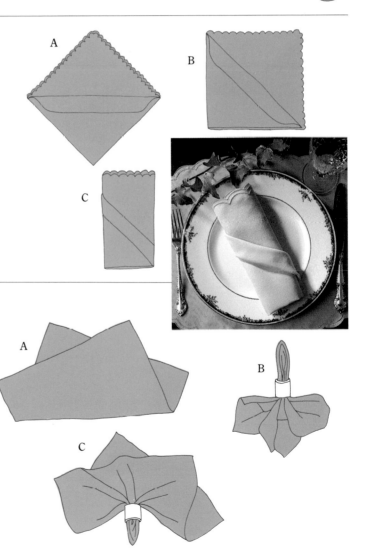

BASIC POSY

A. Lay napkin open and flat. Bring lower right corner up to and beyond top edge, forming two small, equal triangles on either side.

B. Holding napkin in center of bottom edge, loosely pull napkin through a napkin ring, gathering in loose folds.

C. Gently shake napkin to make folds fall attractively.

STATELY FOLD

A. Lay napkin open and flat. Fold napkin in half to form a triangle with points facing down towards you. Fold right point down to bottom point; fold left point down to bottom point.

B. Holding points with your left hand, turn napkin over. Then turn napkin so that open points are at top. Then bring bottom point up to meet top point, forming a triangle.

C. Lift up at center of bottom, and allow napkin to stand up.

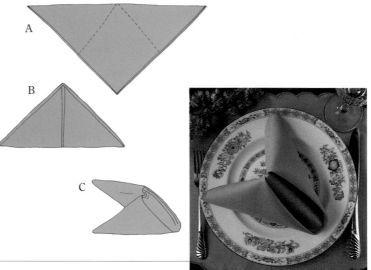

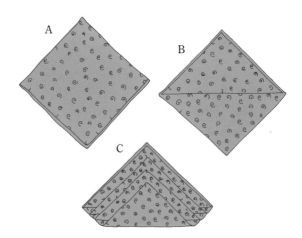

DOUBLE FAN

A. Lay napkin open and flat. Fold in top and bottom edges of napkin so that they meet in middle. Starting with left side, pleat napkin accordian-fashion.

B. Holding pleats together, tie a bow around center with a ribbon.

C. Fan top and bottom pleats out into a circle.

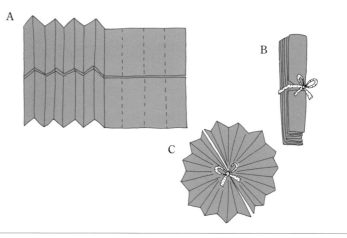

WINGED FOLD

A. Lay napkin open and flat. Fold napkin into quarters with closed corner pointing up and open points pointing down towards you.

B. Starting with bottom point, bring first layer up to meet top point.

C. Bring second layer of bottom point up to within 1 inch of top point. Repeat with remaining two layers. Place on plate with points pointing in desired direction.

STARBURST FOLD

A. Lay napkin open and flat, wrong side up. Fold four corners in sharply so that points meet in center.

B. Fold four new corners in so that they also meet in center. Holding folds in place with your left hand, flip napkin over. Then, again fold in new corners to meet in center. Place napkin in center of plate.

C. Hold napkin corners firmly together in center with your left hand. With your right hand, reach underneath each corner and pick up loose point. Sharply pull each loose point outward. Repeat procedure for each corner and point.

TRIPLE TOWER FOLD

A. Lay napkin open and flat. Fold napkin into a triangle with points facing up. Holding your finger at top point, pull left edge of napkin tight and roll or twist it in towards center.

B. Repeat procedure with right edge. Bring two rolls to within 1 to 2 inches of each other.

C. Fold top point of napkin back and under so that it is equal in length to other two points. Then turn napkin around so that three points are facing away from you.

To emphasize the beautiful grain of a wooden table you may want to consider using place mats rather than covering the table with a tablecloth. Actually, place mats may be used any time you choose not to use a tablecloth, but still want to protect your table from scratches; a runner down the center of the table can also offer some protection. While place mats and runners are typically made from fabric, they are available in almost any material, from mirrors to plastic. For a sparkling contemporary effect, try arranging mirrored mats on a clear glass table. With the addition of crystal, china, and silver, the effect will be dazzling.

Arrange place mats on the table by laying them flush with the table edge or no more than 1½ inches from the edge. It usually looks better if deeply hemmed or fringed mats are placed flush with the table edge. Narrowly hemmed mats, on the other hand, may look better if placed away from the edge. On a round or oval table, lay rectangular mats so that the corner points are flush with the edge. Round mats should also be placed so that their edge is flush with the table edge.

It is rare that tablecloths, napkins, or place mats make it through a dinner party without being soiled or damaged in some way. After all, these items are for guests to use. But since you want to preserve your fine linens and hope to pass them on to your heirs, it is very important that they be laundered properly.

A good rule to remember is to never try to remove a stain, even from an inexpensive napkin, until you have tested a small corner of it to make sure that it is colorfast. If it is a piece of dry-clean-only linen, then limit your effort to sprinkling the fresh stain with cornstarch or salt, allowing it to stand until any liquid is absorbed. If it will be a while before you can take it to the dry cleaners, consider lightly rinsing the stain with cold water. Otherwise, promptly take all dry-clean items to a professional, being sure to point out the stains and explain what caused them.

It is wise to place your name on the underside of tablecloths before they go to the dry cleaners. Unfortunately, this is impossible to do with napkins. Therefore, always be sure to make a list of what napkins are being sent to the cleaners, and check against your list when picking up the linens to make sure the correct number of napkins have been returned to you. You should also make certain that all the napkins are of the same pattern; just imagine how difficult it is for the cleaners to identify all the different patterns in white damask napkins.

Ask the cleaners to return tablecloths without creasing them, if possible. It is better if the cloths are softly folded and placed on a large cardboard roller-hanger or laid out flat and rolled up on a large tube. Napkins should be pressed out flat or folded in half. Place mats should be cleaned, pressed, and stored by laying out smooth and flat.

Washable linens can be laundered at home, but stains may become permanent if not given prompt attention. As soon as guests depart, or even before, if you can discreetly manage it, follow these guidelines for removing stains.

STAIN	TREATMENT
Blood	Soak immediately in cold water, then launder. For white fabrics, add a few drops of ammonia to the water.
Candle wax	Rub with an ice cube until wax hardens; then scrape off with a dull knife. Place napkin between layers of paper towels and press with a warm iron until all wax has been absorbed.
Catsup, tomato sauce, barbecue sauce	Soak immediately in warm water. Then rub spot with detergent and launder, using bleach, if possible.
Coffee	Soak immediately in a solution of one part vinegar to four parts water. Then launder, using bleach, if possible.
Lipstick	Lightly rub with alcohol or glycerine and then rub with detergent. Rinse and launder in lukewarm water.
Red wine	Blot immediately. Sponge with club soda. Rinse in cold water and launder.
Scorch marks	Sponge immediately with club soda. Or sponge with hydrogen peroxide or a solution of one part vinegar to two parts water. Then rinse and launder.
Tea	Soak in a solution of one teaspoon borax to one cup water. Rinse in boiling water. Then launder, using bleach, if possible.
Fruit	Rub stain with salt to absorb the liquid. Blot with vinegar, then launder.
Grease	Blot with dry cleaning fluid. Rinse in hot water. Then rub with detergent and launder.

Through the years, you will probably collect several sets of china. To add more variety to your table settings, try mixing and matching the different patterns and styles.

Dinnerware

Although available in glass and plastic, most dinnerware is either china or earthenware. Both china and earthenware are technically called clayware, since clay is the basic ingredient of both. However, china and earthenware are very different due to the kind and quality of the clays used and their firing temperatures. Generally, earthenware has a softer, more porous body than china and makes a dull sound if tapped. Earthenware is also opaque.

The term "earthenware" includes everything from crude hand-crafted pottery to very fine dinnerware. Pottery dishes are made from coarse, colored clays fired at low temperatures, and they are usually thick and heavy. Pottery dishes are basically not very desirable except for decorative or occasional use; once their glazed surface is broken, the dishes become absorbent and therefore unsafe to eat from. However, pottery made specifically to be used as dinnerware is usually inexpensive and often decorated in unique and sometimes vivid designs.

Finer quality earthenware is made of a lighter clay, flint, or feldspar and is usually fired at a high temperature which makes it more resistant to breaking and chipping. Some fine earthenware is of such high quality that it is semi-translucent. Stoneware is also an earthenware fired at high temperatures and is therefore more durable.

Only fine white clays are used to make china. Although china appears fragile, it is actually more durable than pottery. Fired at higher temperatures than earthenware, china is the most durable of the claywares.

Bone china has traditionally been made only in England. Bone ash is mixed with clay to produce a milky-white, translucent product. It has a soft glaze and mars easily. Belleek china has traditionally been made in Ireland. It is very thin, cream-colored, and translucent. Belleek china has a lustrous gloss that is sometimes iridescent.

Porcelain china, made in the Limoges region of France, is fired at a low temperature first; then a glaze is added. Then it is fired at a high temperature so that the glaze permeates the body for a white, translucent appearance.

Both china and earthenware can be purchased in a wide range of prices. The cost is determined by the kind and quality of the materials used, the amount of decoration, the workmanship, and the lack of defects.

When selecting dinnerware, keep in mind how the pieces will be used, your other table appointments, and the decor of the rooms they will be used in. Always try to visualize the table as it will appear with the dinnerware pattern repeated many times. You may want to consider combining two or three different patterns, some with plain pieces, some with a border, and some with a simple design. This mix-and-match method of selection applies to color, too.

Some dinnerware is available in a variety of colors. Today's hostesses can often afford to acquire several sets of dishes, but bear in mind that a storage area will have to be found for each set that is purchased.

Always store dinnerware carefully to prevent breakage. Line shelves to provide cushioning, and leave room for easy movement in and out cabinets. Separate stacked plates with napkins or paper towels, and never stack more than two cups together. Cover dishes that are used infrequently to prevent them from becoming dusty and greasy.

If you like for plates to be warm at serving time, remember that earthenware should be placed only in a barely warm oven. If overheated, the glaze may crack, causing the plate to break. When rinsing and scraping dinnerware, use a rubber spatula or a soft cloth. Never allow dirty dinnerware to stand too long without rinsing, since stains on earthenware can be difficult to remove. Hand wash in warm water with a mild detergent, and rinse with hot water; dry with a lint-free cloth or let air-dry.

Today many china manufacturers say that fine china is dishwasher-safe. However, hand-painted, over-the-glaze decorations and gold and platinum trim cannot withstand the intense heat of the dishwasher, so they should be hand washed. When loading the dishwasher, alternate plates of various sizes to avoid scratching and chipping.

If you do have some breakage and your pattern has been discontinued, try contacting a tracing company. Given time, such companies can often locate a source for replacing broken or missing pieces.

Protect your china investments by storing the pieces carefully. Never stack pieces haphazardly; covering in protective wrappers with padding between each piece will prevent a dusty, oily film from developing.

Glassware

Although we use paper or plastic cups from time to time, we all seem to prefer the beauty of fine glassware. It glistens, glimmers, and reflects the glow of candles with splendor. The two main types of beverage glassware that appear on the dining table are lime glass and lead glass.

Lime glass is made from sand, soda, lime, and other materials that add clarity or color. This glass is hard, but brittle, and therefore does not lend itself to cut-type designs. Many tumblers and glass dishes are made from it.

Sand, potash, lime, and lead oxide make up lead glass. This type of glass is soft and scratches easily, but it has brilliant shine and reflecting qualities. Full-lead crystal contains at least 33⅓ percent lead oxide.

The process of mouth blowing lead crystal stemware is often replaced by machines. Machine-made pieces are created more quickly and are more uniform in shape, while mouth-blown crystal goblets have slight irregularities. Prices are usually more reasonable for the machine-made crystal pieces.

Lead crystal can be cut, etched, tinted, or rimmed with gold or platinum. Any etching should be crisp and neat; cut areas should be clean and smooth. Another test is to lightly flick the bowl of a goblet with your fingernail; the brighter the tone, the better the quality of the crystal. When selecting stemware, look for patterns that have been around awhile so that you will be able to add to your set later or replace broken pieces. However, there is never a guarantee that a pattern will not be discontinued.

Hand washing is recommended for crystal stemware, particularly those pieces trimmed with gold or platinum. To prevent chipping and breaking, use a plastic dishpan or line the bottom of your sink with a rubber mat or towel. Always remove your rings and bracelets to avoid scratching the glasses, and wash and rinse one piece at a time. Because drastic temperature changes may cause crystal to crack, never place ice-cold glasses in hot dishwater.

Undecorated and thicker crystal can be washed in the dishwasher. When loading, leave room between stemware pieces, and secure each piece between the cushioned prongs on the top rack. Both automatic and hand dishwashing detergents are safe for most crystal. However, sometimes a cloudy white film is produced when dishwasher detergents and softened water come in contact with certain types of glassware. To avoid this, you may choose to wash fine glassware by hand.

Always store crystal stemware right side up to avoid placing unnecessary pressure on the rim. For added protection, line shelves with a soft cloth. If crystal should develop a cloudy look when stored over a long period of time, try rubbing it with lemon juice and then wash in vinegar or use a foaming denture cleaner in the water. If you are unable to remove the cloudy appearance, take the crystal to a professional for an acid bath.

If crystal is slightly chipped on an edge, try using an emery board to lightly smooth the damaged area; otherwise, seek professional repair help. Many times, the chipped edge of a crystal glass can be professionally ground to create a new smooth edge, thus saving the glass. Repairmen for this task may be difficult to find, but often your local jeweler can suggest a source.

To remove stains from crystal bowls and vases, soak them in a solution of ammonia or bleach and water or soak in water in which you have dissolved a denture cleaning tablet. Crystal decanters are best soaked in a vinegar and water solution when trying to dissolve wine sediment; a small amount of uncooked rice swished around in the decanter will act as a mild abrasive to help remove the stains.

Flatware and Holloware

Beautiful flatware certainly helps make a prettier table. Flatware is currently available in a variety of materials: sterling silver, silver-plate, vermeil, stainless steel, and such novel combinations as metal with bone, bamboo, plastic, ceramic, or mother-of-pearl handles.

Pieces that are marked "sterling" or "sterling silver" are made from an alloy of silver and another metal, often copper. These pieces consist of mostly silver, but the addition

Lead crystal should be handled gently and lovingly. For extra shine, cleanse with a solution of ammonia or bleach and water.

of a second metal adds hardness and durability. Pieces made of solid silver are soft and can be dented easily.

The durability of sterling flatware is usually determined by its weight. The heavier the flatware, the longer it will last; however, even lightweight silver flatware will provide years and years of service. In general, the heavier sterling is more expensive. The same is true for the more intricately designed and hand-finished pieces.

Sterling flatware is usually sold in four-piece place settings that include the dinner knife, fork, salad fork, and teaspoon. A tablespoon is included if sold as a five-piece place setting; in a six-piece place setting, the butter spreader makes the sixth piece. At first, it may seem overwhelming to determine the uses of all the different pieces of flatware, but just remember that table settings are based on nothing more than common sense and three basic pieces of eating equipment—knives, forks, and spoons.

Silver-plated flatware is composed of a core of base metal coated with silver. The silver is usually added by an electroplating process. The quality of silver-plated flatware is determined by the kind of base metal used, the amount of silver applied, and the quality of workmanship. Always check to see what base metal is used; flatware plated over steel may rust when the silver begins to wear off unless the steel has been alloyed and is rust resistant.

Stainless steel, made of chrome and nickel, has the advantage of being tarnish- and scratch-resistant. Several different grades of stainless are available; the economy grade may tend to have rough edges. The higher grades have been polished to a soft, permanent luster.

Vermeil is gold-plated flatware. Originally, vermeil was gold-plate over sterling silver. However, today it is applied not only to sterling silver but also to stainless steel. The result is a warm-colored, non-tarnishing flatware.

Trays, pitchers, vases, and other pieces used for serving food or for decoration are called holloware. Hollow pieces are usually available in sterling, silver-plate, vermeil, stainless steel, pewter, copper, and brass.

Sterling holloware pieces come in different weights. Lightweight pieces can be dented easily. Some lightweight pieces have weighted bases, which make them feel heavier. If the pieces are weighted, this information should be stamped on the bottom. Silver-plated holloware is harder than sterling and less easily dented. The price for each varies according to the amount of silver used, the weight, and the workmanship.

Holloware made from stainless steel can withstand high temperatures and does not tarnish. Pewter is also practical in that it tarnishes slowly. But fine sterling and silver-plated flatware and holloware require particular care. Contact with

The modern flatware purchase is ordinarily eight to twelve place settings consisting of four to six pieces each. But antique sterling place settings often included many utensils of various shapes and sizes for every kind of food imaginable.

Don't let large pieces of holloware tarnish and collect dust in cabinets; use them in decorations. Here, a silver casserole, supported by a pedestal base, holds a lovely flower arrangement.

any form of rubber and the reaction of the sulfur in the air with eggs, mayonnaise, and mustard will tarnish silver. Moist salt can also cause spots and corrosion. If the corrosion is allowed to remain for a period of time, it will eat into the silver. Never store salt in a silver or silver-plated salt cellar, nor in a crystal one that has a silver or silver-plated top.

Don't be afraid to use your silver flatware on a daily basis, because when silver is used often, it develops a wonderful patina. However, it is important to know how to clean silver properly. Always wash or rinse soon after using; soaking in water for several hours will dull the finish and loosen knife handles. For best results, hand-wash silver in hot water, using a mild detergent and a soft cloth. Always dry thoroughly; do not allow pieces to air-dry in a rubber dish drainer or on a rubber tray.

You may use automatic dishwashers to wash silver if your detergent does not contain bleaching agents. Bleaching agents remove the oxidation that highlights silver. Be sure to load the dishwasher with the handles of the silver flatware pointing down, and spread pieces out to prevent scratching. Your pieces will also look better if they are removed from the dishwasher before the drying cycle begins and hand-dried or buffed.

Tarnished spots should be cleaned as soon as possible. A non-abrasive silver cleaner and a soft-bristled brush for hard-to-reach areas should be helpful. Never lacquer or plastic-coat silver; the coatings will eventually darken and flake or chip off.

Proper storage of flatware and holloware protects it from scratches and air. Use special tarnish-proof cloths, cotton bags, or cotton flannel-lined cabinets. When stacking, use a soft material between the pieces for protection.

Flatware and holloware are precious investments. Knowing how to care for the pieces will extend their life and allow you and your family many years of enjoyment.

Menus
for
Entertaining

Whether entertaining two or twelve, the information in this section of the book will help you decide how to cook and present the meal you have chosen.

While the photographs will lead you to think about the visual aspects of entertaining, it is the recipes that will form the heart of the meal. The menu themes are created with home entertaining in mind, so you may want to use each menu in its entirety, or you may elect to mix and match the menus and recipes.

To use the menus to their best advantage, it is important to understand that the wine selections are listed following the food course or courses they are to accompany. In other words, the recipes listed above each wine can be served with that particular wine. However, if the beverage—either wine, water, tea, or coffee—is listed last and set apart from the rest of the courses, then it can be served with the entire menu. Also note that the menu courses appear in this order: appetizer, soup, salad, entrée, side dishes, bread, and dessert. Enjoy!

The following menus are designed to take the panic out of entertaining. The occasions range from sophisticated dinners to casual suppers and picnics. Adapt the recipes and decorating ideas to meet your own needs, and your gatherings will be dramatic, delicious, and enjoyable.

Fireside Feast

When it's cold outside, set up an array of tables, chairs, and pillows and entertain inside, in front of a blazing fire. Begin the evening with Tapenade and Three Apple Salad with Radicchio. Hearty Osso Buco with Orzo Milanese is ideal for chilly weather, especially when accompanied by Glazed Leeks, Poppyseed Rolls, and a spicy, earthy-flavored red wine. Guests will linger over Individual Orange Flans; they are superb served with a rich, very sweet sauterne.

Fireside Feast

Tapenade

Three Apple Salad with Radicchio

Osso Buco with Orzo Milanese

Glazed Leeks

Poppyseed Rolls

Château de Beaucastel

Individual Orange Flans

Montrose Sauterne

Coffee

Water

Serves six

Tapenade

¾ cup chopped fresh parsley
½ cup pitted ripe olives
¼ cup salad olives
¼ cup chopped fresh basil
3 anchovy fillets, rinsed and
   drained
2 tablespoons capers
1 clove garlic
1 tablespoon lemon juice
⅛ teaspoon coarsely ground
   pepper
¼ cup olive oil
1 large sweet red pepper
Belgian endive leaves
Red pepper strips
Carrot sticks

Position knife blade in food processor bowl. Combine first 9 ingredients in processor bowl. Top with cover, and process until mixture is smooth, scraping sides of bowl occasionally. Slowly pour olive oil through food chute with processor running; process 2 minutes or until mixture thickens, scraping sides of bowl occasionally.

Cut off top of red pepper; remove seeds. Cut a thin slice from the bottom of red pepper, if necessary, so that pepper stands upright. Spoon dip into pepper cup. Serve with endive, red pepper strips, and carrot sticks. Yield: 1 cup.

Three Apple Salad with Radicchio

1 large Red Delicious apple, unpeeled and diced
1 large Golden Delicious apple, unpeeled and diced
1 large Granny Smith apple, unpeeled and diced
½ teaspoon ascorbic-citric powder
¼ pound seedless red grapes, halved
¼ pound seedless green grapes, halved
½ cup coarsely chopped pecans
½ cup finely diced celery
⅓ cup golden raisins
¼ cup plus 2 tablespoons mayonnaise
Radicchio leaves

Combine apples in a large mixing bowl; sprinkle with ascorbic-citric powder, and toss gently. Add grapes, pecans, celery, raisins, and mayonnaise; stir well. Spoon mixture onto radicchio-lined salad plates. Yield: 6 servings.

Osso Buco with Orzo Milanese

6 (1½- to 2-inch-thick) veal shanks (about 1 pound each)
All-purpose flour
3 tablespoons olive oil
1 cup diced carrot
1 cup chopped celery
1 cup chopped onion
1 large clove garlic, minced
1 (28-ounce) can plum tomatoes, undrained and chopped
1 cup Chablis or other dry white wine
½ cup water
¼ cup minced fresh parsley
1 bay leaf
1½ teaspoons beef-flavored bouillon granules
1 teaspoon dried whole basil
½ teaspoon salt
½ teaspoon dried whole oregano
¼ teaspoon garlic powder
⅛ teaspoon coarsely ground pepper
Orzo Milanese
¼ cup water
2 tablespoons all-purpose flour
2 tablespoons minced fresh parsley
1 teaspoon grated lemon rind

Using kitchen twine, tie each veal shank in two places (package-fashion) to keep shape. Dredge shanks in flour; brown in hot oil in a Dutch oven. Remove veal from Dutch oven, reserving drippings. Add carrot, celery, onion, and minced garlic to drippings. Cook, uncovered, until vegetables are tender. Drain off drippings. Return veal to Dutch oven with vegetables. Add tomatoes and next 10 ingredients. Bring mixture to a boil; cover, reduce heat, and simmer 2 to 2½ hours or until veal is tender. Remove and discard bay leaf.

Arrange veal over Orzo Milanese on a serving platter; remove and discard twine. Combine ¼ cup water and 2 tablespoons flour, stirring well; add to tomato mixture, and cook until thickened. Pour over veal; sprinkle with 2 tablespoons parsley and lemon rind. Yield: 6 servings.

Orzo Milanese

¼ cup chopped onion
1 teaspoon butter or margarine, melted
1 cup water
1 cup Chablis or other dry white wine
2 teaspoons beef-flavored bouillon granules
¼ teaspoon ground saffron
1 cup uncooked orzo

Sauté chopped onion in butter in a medium saucepan over medium heat until tender. Add water, wine, bouillon granules, and saffron; bring to a boil. Add orzo; return mixture to a boil. Cover, reduce heat to medium low, and simmer 10 minutes or until orzo is tender. Drain, if necessary, and serve immediately. Yield: 6 servings.

Glazed Leeks

12 small leeks
¼ cup butter or margarine
¼ cup firmly packed brown sugar
3 tablespoons lemon juice

Remove roots, tough outer leaves, and tops from leeks; wash leeks thoroughly. Place leeks in a large skillet; cover and cook in a small amount of boiling salted water 6 to 8 minutes or just until tender. Drain; remove leeks from skillet, and set aside.

Combine butter, sugar, and lemon juice in skillet; cook over low heat, stirring constantly, until sugar dissolves. Return leeks to skillet, and cook over low heat just until glazed, stirring occasionally. Serve with a slotted spoon. Yield: 6 servings.

The smooth, creamy texture and not-too-sweet taste makes Individual Orange Flans a pleasing dessert.

Poppyseed Rolls

2 packages dry yeast
2 cups warm water (105° to 115°)
2 teaspoons sugar
1 teaspoon salt

4 to 5 cups all-purpose flour
2 tablespoons butter or
  margarine, melted
Poppyseeds

Dissolve yeast in warm water; let stand 5 minutes. Add sugar and salt; stir well. Gradually stir in enough flour to make a soft dough.

Turn dough out onto a lightly floured surface, and knead until smooth and elastic (about 8 to 10 minutes). Place in a well-greased bowl, turning to grease top. Cover and let rise in a warm place (85°), free from drafts, 45 minutes or until doubled in bulk.

Punch dough down, and shape into 18 (3½- x 1½-inch) loaf-shaped rolls; place on greased baking sheets. Using a sharp knife, make ¼-inch-deep slashes in tops of rolls. Brush with butter; sprinkle with poppyseeds. Cover and let rise in a warm place, free from drafts, 30 minutes or until doubled in bulk. Bake at 400° for 20 to 25 minutes or until golden. Yield: 1½ dozen.

Individual Orange Flans

½ cup sugar
2 teaspoons hot water
2 cups milk
3 eggs
½ cup sugar

1 teaspoon Grand Marnier or
  other orange-flavored liqueur
½ teaspoon orange extract
Dash of salt
Grated orange rind

Place ½ cup sugar in a heavy saucepan over medium heat. Shake pan and stir occasionally until sugar melts and turns a light golden brown. Remove from heat; add water, stirring well. Pour hot caramel mixture into six 6-ounce custard cups, tipping each cup quickly to coat bottom evenly. Let cool (mixture may harden and crack slightly as it cools).

Place milk in top of a double boiler; bring water to a boil. Cook until milk is thoroughly heated (do not boil). Set aside. Beat eggs until frothy. Add ½ cup sugar and next 3 ingredients; beat well. Gradually stir about ½ cup hot milk into egg mixture; add to remaining milk, stirring constantly.

Pour egg mixture evenly into custard cups. Place cups in a 13- x 9- x 2-inch baking dish; add hot water to a depth of 1 inch into dish. Bake at 350° for 45 to 50 minutes or until a knife inserted in center of custard comes out clean. Remove cups from water; cool. Chill flans 2 to 3 hours. To serve, loosen edges of custards with a spatula, and invert onto individual dessert plates. Sprinkle with grated orange rind. Yield: 6 servings.

Dazzling
Seafood
Dinner

A show of city lights will dazzle guests when they join you for this seafood dinner. The menu features Refreshing Margaritas and Coastal Fried Oysters with Cocktail Dipping Sauce, followed by Asparagus Fan Salad, Crabmeat Imperials, Pasta with Parsley, Garlic, and Basil Sauce, and Sautéed Carrots and Radishes. Then adjourn to the living room and relax in style with Pink Pears with Grated Chocolate.

Dazzling Seafood Dinner

Refreshing Margaritas

Coastal Fried Oysters with
Cocktail Dipping Sauce

Asparagus Fan Salad

Crabmeat Imperials

Pasta with Parsley, Garlic, and
Basil Sauce

Sautéed Carrots and Radishes

Pink Pears with Grated Chocolate

Coffee

Water

Serves six

Refreshing Margaritas

Lime wedges
Salt
**2 (6-ounce) cans frozen limeade
    concentrate, thawed and
    undiluted**
1 cup tequila
**⅔ cup Triple Sec or other
    orange-flavored liqueur**
2 tablespoons powdered sugar
Ice cubes
Lime slices

Rub rims of cocktail glasses with wedges of lime. Place salt in a saucer; spin rim of each glass in salt. Set prepared glasses aside.

Combine 1 can limeade concentrate, ½ cup tequila, ⅓ cup liqueur, and 1 tablespoon powdered sugar in container of an electric blender; top with cover, and process until smooth. Add enough ice cubes to make mixture measure 3½ cups in blender; blend well.

Pour beverage into prepared glasses; garnish with lime slices. Repeat procedure with remaining ingredients. Yield: 7 cups.

Arrange tender asparagus spears and tomato wedges into this fan-shaped salad. A dollop of tangy dressing forms the base of each salad.

Coastal Fried Oysters with Cocktail Dipping Sauce

3 eggs, beaten
⅓ cup milk
½ teaspoon salt
3 (12-ounce) containers fresh Standard oysters, drained
1 cup all-purpose flour
4 cups soft breadcrumbs
Vegetable oil
Cocktail Dipping Sauce

Combine beaten eggs, milk, and salt in a large bowl, and stir well. Dip oysters in egg mixture. Dredge oysters in flour; dip in egg mixture again, and coat evenly with breadcrumbs. Let breaded oysters stand 10 minutes.

Fry oysters in hot oil (375°) for 2 to 3 minutes or until browned. Drain on paper towels. Serve with Cocktail Dipping Sauce. Yield: 6 servings.

Cocktail Dipping Sauce

½ cup chili sauce
½ cup catsup
3 tablespoons lemon juice
1 tablespoon prepared horseradish
1 teaspoon white wine Worcestershire sauce
½ teaspoon grated onion
¼ teaspoon garlic salt
⅛ teaspoon hot sauce

Combine all ingredients in a small bowl; stir well. Cover and chill thoroughly. Yield: 1¼ cups.

Asparagus Fan Salad

1½ pounds fresh asparagus spears
3 large tomatoes
1 egg
1 egg yolk
1 tablespoon plus 1½ teaspoons lemon juice, divided
¼ teaspoon garlic salt
½ cup plus 2 tablespoons olive oil
¼ cup loosely packed fresh basil leaves
3 fresh mint leaves
½ teaspoon grated lemon rind

Snap off tough ends of asparagus. Remove scales from stalks with a knife, if desired. Arrange asparagus in a vegetable steamer over boiling water. Cover and steam 6 minutes or until crisp-tender; drain. Rinse with cold water; drain.

Cut each tomato into 8 wedges. Arrange asparagus in a fan shape on salad plates. Place 4 tomato wedges in a fan shape at base of asparagus.

Position knife blade in food processor bowl; add egg, egg yolk, 1 tablespoon lemon juice, and garlic salt. Process 20 seconds or until smooth. With processor running, pour oil through food chute in a slow, steady stream; process until thickened. Add basil, mint, and lemon rind. Process until herbs are finely chopped. Add remaining 1½ teaspoons lemon juice; process until blended. Place a dollop of mayonnaise mixture at base of each salad. Yield: 6 servings.

Crabmeat Imperials

⅓ cup chopped green pepper
¼ cup chopped green onions
3 tablespoons diced celery
1 (2-ounce) jar diced pimiento, drained
3 tablespoons butter or margarine, melted
1 tablespoon chopped fresh parsley
1 teaspoon Beau Monde seasoning
½ teaspoon prepared horseradish
½ teaspoon white wine Worcestershire sauce
¼ teaspoon Dijon mustard
¼ teaspoon hot sauce
1 egg, beaten
¼ cup plus 2 tablespoons mayonnaise
1½ pounds fresh lump crabmeat, drained
Pimiento strips (optional)
Celery leaves (optional)

Sauté green pepper, onions, celery, and diced pimiento in butter in a large skillet until tender. Stir in parsley, Beau Monde seasoning, horseradish, Worcestershire sauce, mustard, and hot sauce. Remove from heat, and set aside.

Combine egg and mayonnaise; stir in green pepper mixture. Gently stir in crabmeat. Spoon mixture into 6 baking shells. Bake at 375° for 12 to 15 minutes. Broil 2 to 3 minutes or until tops are lightly browned. If desired, garnish with pimiento strips and celery leaves. Yield: 6 servings.

Pasta with Parsley, Garlic, and Basil Sauce

12 ounces linguine, uncooked
2 cloves garlic, minced
2 teaspoons olive oil
1 cup grated Parmesan cheese
½ cup butter or margarine, softened
½ cup whipping cream
¼ cup chopped fresh parsley
1 to 2 tablespoons minced fresh basil
¼ teaspoon white pepper

Cook linguine according to package directions, omitting salt. Drain well; place in a large bowl. Set aside, and keep warm.

Sauté garlic in olive oil until lightly browned. Pour over hot pasta. Add Parmesan cheese and remaining ingredients, tossing until pasta is coated and butter is melted. Yield: 6 servings.

Sautéed Carrots and Radishes

3 tablespoons butter or margarine
2½ cups thinly sliced carrots
1¼ cups thinly sliced radishes
   (about 6 ounces)
¼ teaspoon sugar
½ teaspoon salt
¼ teaspoon coarsely ground
   pepper

Melt butter in a large skillet over medium heat. Add carrots, and sauté 5 to 6 minutes; add radishes and sugar. Sauté an additional 5 minutes or until vegetables are tender. Sprinkle with salt and pepper; serve immediately. Yield: 6 servings.

Pink Pears with Grated Chocolate

6 medium pears
¾ cup sugar
1½ cups water
1½ cups rosé wine
½ cup Burgundy or other dry red
   wine
1 teaspoon lemon juice
4 whole cloves
1 (3-inch) stick cinnamon
Grated semisweet chocolate

Peel pears, removing core from bottom end and cutting to, but not through, the stem end. Slice ¼ inch from bottom of each pear to make a flat base. Set pears aside.

Combine sugar and next 6 ingredients in a 5-quart Dutch oven; bring to a boil over medium heat, stirring until sugar dissolves. Place pears in Dutch oven in an upright position; spoon syrup over pears. Cover and simmer 20 minutes.

Transfer pears to a large bowl. Strain syrup, and pour over pears, discarding spices. Cover and refrigerate pears 2 to 3 hours, basting occasionally with syrup.

Spoon pears and syrup into a serving dish; sprinkle with grated chocolate. Yield: 6 servings.

For delicately flavored Pink Pears with Grated Chocolate, poach the pears in a mixture of rosé and Burgundy wines.

Romantic Celebration

Select a quiet, intimate setting for this romantic dinner for two. Tempt appetites with Pecan-Fried Cheese and a dry white wine. Dinner officially begins with pretty Beet and Potato Salad; Roasted Baby Lamb Chops with Mint Dressing, Couscous with Curry and Pine Nuts, Zucchini and Sun-Dried Tomatoes, and a spicy, velvety red wine follow. The desserts, Sweet Oranges with Cracked Sugar and Orange Cookies, are guaranteed to make this an occasion to remember.

Romantic Celebration

Pecan-Fried Cheese

Murphy-Goode Chardonnay

———

Beet and Potato Salad

Roasted Baby Lamb Chops with
Mint Dressing

Couscous with Curry and Pine Nuts

Zucchini and Sun-Dried Tomatoes

Saintsbury Pinot Noir

———

Sweet Oranges with Cracked Sugar

Orange Cookies

Coffee

———

Water

Serves two

Pecan-Fried Cheese

⅓ cup pecans, toasted and
  ground
2 tablespoons fine, dry
  breadcrumbs
1 egg, beaten
1 tablespoon milk
1 (4½-ounce) round, fully ripened
  Brie cheese
2 tablespoons all-purpose flour
Vegetable oil

Combine pecans and bread-
crumbs. Combine egg and milk. Dip
Brie in egg mixture; dredge in flour.
Dip again in egg mixture; dredge in
pecan mixture, coating cheese completely. Place cheese on wax paper;
cover and chill at least 30 minutes.
Fry cheese in hot oil (350°) for 1 to 2
minutes or until lightly browned.
Serve warm with assorted crackers.
Yield: one cheese round.

Beet and Potato Salad

¼ cup vegetable oil
2 tablespoons white wine vinegar
1 tablespoon dry white wine
¼ teaspoon salt
¼ teaspoon white pepper
2 small fresh beets with leaves
⅔ pound small new potatoes, unpeeled
1 green onion, chopped
1 tablespoon chopped fresh parsley
8 Boston lettuce leaves

Combine first 5 ingredients, stirring well. Set aside.

Remove leaves from beets, leaving 1 inch of stems. Place beets in a small saucepan; add water to cover. Bring water to a boil; cover, reduce heat, and simmer 20 to 30 minutes or just until beets are tender. Drain. Pour cold water over beets, and drain again; cool. Peel and dice beets; set aside.

Place potatoes in a large saucepan; add water to cover. Bring water to a boil; cover, reduce heat, and simmer 15 to 20 minutes or just until potatoes are tender. Drain and cool slightly. Peel and dice potatoes; set aside.

Stir vinegar mixture again, and pour over potatoes; sprinkle with green onion and parsley. Toss gently; let cool. Line salad plates with lettuce leaves. Just before serving, gently add beets to potato mixture. Serve immediately over lettuce leaves. Yield: 2 servings.

Roasted Baby Lamb Chops with Mint Dressing

1 (1¼-pound) Frenched 6- to 7-bone baby rack of lamb
¾ teaspoon grated fresh gingerroot
¼ teaspoon dried whole rosemary
1 to 2 cups apple cider
1 tablespoon honey
¼ teaspoon coarsely ground pepper
Mint Dressing

Rub meaty portion of lamb with gingerroot and rosemary. Place lamb in an aluminum foil-lined shallow roasting pan; add cider to pan. Bake at 450° for 10 minutes. Drizzle honey over lamb; bake an additional 10 to 12 minutes or to desired degree of doneness. Place lamb on a serving platter, and sprinkle with pepper. Cover with aluminum foil; let stand 10 minutes. Carve lamb into individual chops. Serve with Mint Dressing. Yield: 2 servings.

Mint Dressing

2 tablespoons brown sugar
¼ cup vinegar
2 tablespoons water
¼ cup plus 2 tablespoons apple jelly
¼ cup minced fresh mint leaves

Combine first 3 ingredients in a saucepan; cook over medium heat, stirring occasionally, until mixture is reduced by one-third. Stir in jelly; cook over low heat until melted. Stir in mint. Cool completely. Yield: ¾ cup.

Fresh beets and new potatoes form this pretty salad. The colorful mixture is dressed with a tangy vinaigrette.

Couscous with Curry and Pine Nuts

2 tablespoons sliced green onions
2 tablespoons butter or
  margarine, melted
½ cup water
¼ teaspoon chicken-flavored
  bouillon granules
½ cup uncooked couscous
2 tablespoons pine nuts
¼ teaspoon curry powder
⅛ teaspoon ground allspice

Sauté green onions in butter in a small saucepan until tender. Add water; bring mixture to a boil. Stir in bouillon granules. Add couscous and remaining ingredients, stirring well. Cover, remove from heat, and let stand 5 minutes or until liquid is absorbed. Fluff couscous with a fork before serving. Yield: 2 servings.

Zucchini and Sun-Dried Tomatoes

1 cup water
¾ cup (1 ounce) coarsely chopped
  sun-dried tomatoes
2 small zucchini, thinly sliced
1 tablespoon olive oil
½ teaspoon sugar
½ teaspoon salt
¼ teaspoon dried Italian
  seasoning
⅛ teaspoon pepper

Bring water to a boil in a small saucepan. Add tomatoes; reduce heat, and simmer 4 minutes. Drain tomatoes well; set aside. Sauté sliced zucchini in olive oil in a skillet 3 minutes; add tomatoes, sugar, and remaining ingredients. Cook 2 minutes or until zucchini is crisp-tender, stirring frequently. Serve warm. Yield: 2 servings.

Sweet Oranges with Cracked Sugar

¼ cup sugar
1½ teaspoons water
2 navel oranges
3 tablespoons Grand Marnier or
  other orange-flavored liqueur
¾ teaspoon minced crystallized
  ginger
⅓ cup whipping cream
1 teaspoon powdered sugar

Combine ¼ cup sugar and water in a small heavy saucepan. Cook over medium heat until sugar dissolves and mixture caramelizes and turns golden brown. Pour mixture onto a foil-lined baking sheet. Tilt baking sheet to spread mixture to ¼-inch thickness. Cool completely; break mixture into bite-size pieces.
Peel oranges, removing outer membrane. Cut crosswise into slices, and place in a shallow dish. Sprinkle oranges with Grand Marnier and crystallized ginger; chill 1 hour. Combine whipping cream and powdered sugar in a medium mixing bowl; beat at medium speed of an electric mixer until stiff peaks form. To serve, spoon oranges and Grand Marnier into serving dishes. Top with whipped cream, and sprinkle with sugar mixture. Yield: 2 servings.

Orange Cookies

1 cup shortening
1 cup sugar
1 egg
1 tablespoon grated orange rind
1 tablespoon orange juice
2¼ cups all-purpose flour
1 teaspoon baking powder
Pinch of salt
1 cup chopped pecans

Cream shortening; gradually add sugar, beating at medium speed of an electric mixer until light and fluffy. Add egg, orange rind, and orange juice; beat well.
Combine flour, baking powder, and salt. Add to creamed mixture, beating just until blended. Stir in pecans. Shape dough into a 15-inch-long roll; wrap in wax paper, and chill 2 hours or until dough is firm.
Unwrap roll, and cut into ¼-inch slices; place on lightly greased cookie sheets. Bake at 375° for 15 to 17 minutes or until lightly browned. Cool on wire racks. Yield: 3 dozen.

Sweet Oranges with Cracked Sugar looks elegant but is very easy to prepare. The fresh citrus flavor of this dessert teams nicely with crisp Orange Cookies.

Dinner Before the Symphony

This glass table looks exotic when graced with soft light, tropical flowers, and large leaf place mats. Introduce guests over Best Baked Brie and a light white wine. Bibb and Watercress Salad with Champagne Dressing is followed by Fruit- and Nut-Stuffed Pork Chops, Glazed Julienne of Carrots, Turnips, and Rutabagas, Cherry Tomatoes with Feta Cheese, and French Bread Rolls. A full-bodied, fruity red wine accompanies the menu. Be sure guests sample sinfully rich White Chocolate Mousse before departing for the evening.

Dinner Before the Symphony

Best Baked Brie

Muscadet de Sèvre et Maine, Sur Lie

Bibb and Watercress Salad with
Champagne Dressing

Fruit- and Nut-Stuffed Pork Chops

Glazed Julienne of Carrots, Turnips,
and Rutabagas

Cherry Tomatoes with Feta Cheese

French Bread Rolls

Ridge California Zinfandel, York Creek

White Chocolate Mousse

Coffee

Water

Serves six

Best Baked Brie

2 (10- x 9-inch) sheets
   commercial frozen puff pastry,
   thawed
1 (15-ounce) round, fully ripened
   Brie cheese
1 (4.5-ounce) package strawberry-
   or cherry-flavored Neufchâtel
   cheese, softened
1 egg, beaten
1 tablespoon water
Thin gingersnaps

   Lightly flour baking sheet. Place 1
sheet of pastry on baking sheet, and
gently roll out to remove fold lines.
Place Brie in center of pastry.
Spread half of Neufchâtel cheese on
Brie. Turn Brie over; spread with
remaining Neufchâtel. Bring pastry
up and over cheese, wrapping completely; place seam side down on
baking sheet.
   Cut decorative designs out of remaining sheet of pastry; place on top
of pastry-covered Brie.
   Combine egg and water; brush
over top. Bake at 375° for 20 to 25
minutes or until pastry is golden
brown. Let stand 5 to 10 minutes;
serve warm with gingersnaps. Yield:
one cheese round.

*When guests arrive, offer Best Baked Brie
with gingersnaps along with a light, fruity
white wine.*

Bibb and Watercress Salad with Champagne Dressing

1 medium-size green pepper, diced
1 medium cucumber, peeled and diced
½ cup sliced green onions
24 Bibb lettuce leaves (about 2 heads)
12 radicchio leaves (about 1 head)
1 cup torn watercress
1 egg yolk
3 tablespoons champagne vinegar
1 teaspoon Dijon mustard
⅛ teaspoon salt
⅛ teaspoon coarsely ground pepper
½ cup plus 2 tablespoons vegetable oil

Combine green pepper, cucumber, and onions, tossing gently. Arrange 4 Bibb lettuce leaves and 2 radicchio leaves on each individual salad plate; spoon vegetable mixture in center. Sprinkle with watercress.

Combine egg yolk, vinegar, mustard, salt, and pepper in container of an electric blender. Top with cover, and process 1 minute. With blender on high, gradually add oil in a slow, steady stream, processing until blended. Serve dressing over salad. Yield: 6 servings.

Fruit- and Nut-Stuffed Pork Chops

1½ cups toasted ½-inch white bread cubes
½ cup peeled, chopped apple
⅓ cup (1.3 ounces) shredded sharp Cheddar cheese
2 tablespoons finely chopped pecans, toasted
¼ teaspoon salt
⅛ teaspoon ground cinnamon
2 tablespoons butter or margarine, melted
6 (1¼-inch-thick) pork chops, cut with pockets
½ teaspoon salt
¼ teaspoon pepper
½ cup seasoned dry breadcrumbs
½ cup orange juice

Combine bread cubes, apple, cheese, pecans, ¼ teaspoon salt, and cinnamon. Add butter; stir until bread cubes are lightly coated.

Sprinkle pocket of pork chops with ½ teaspoon salt and pepper; stuff with bread cube mixture. Dredge pork chops in seasoned breadcrumbs. Place chops in a 13- x 9- x 2-inch baking dish; pour orange juice around chops. Cover and bake at 350° for 30 minutes. Uncover and bake an additional 30 minutes. Remove pork chops from baking dish, and serve immediately. Yield: 6 servings.

Glazed Julienne of Carrots, Turnips, and Rutabagas

¾ pound carrots, scraped and cut into 1½-inch julienne strips
¾ pound turnips, peeled and cut into 1½-inch julienne strips
½ pound rutabaga, peeled and cut into 1½-inch julienne strips
3 tablespoons butter or margarine
2 tablespoons sugar
2 tablespoons water
¼ teaspoon salt
⅛ teaspoon pepper

Combine all ingredients in a large skillet, and bring to a boil. Cover, reduce heat to low, and cook 10 to 12 minutes or until vegetables are crisp-tender. Serve immediately. Yield: 6 servings.

Cherry Tomatoes with Feta Cheese

1 pint small cherry tomatoes, halved
1 cup (4 ounces) crumbled feta cheese
⅓ cup olive oil
⅓ cup wine vinegar
½ teaspoon dried whole oregano
½ teaspoon dried whole thyme
¼ teaspoon salt

Combine tomatoes and cheese in a medium bowl. Combine remaining ingredients in a jar. Cover tightly, and shake vigorously. Pour dressing over tomato mixture, tossing gently. Cover and chill at least 2 hours. Serve with a slotted spoon. Yield: 6 servings.

French Bread Rolls

3½ cups all-purpose flour
1½ teaspoons salt
1 package dry yeast
1 cup water
¼ cup milk
2 tablespoons butter or margarine
Cornmeal

Combine flour, salt, and yeast in a large mixing bowl; stir well. Combine water, milk, and butter in a saucepan; heat until butter melts, stirring occasionally. Cool milk mixture to 120° to 130°.

Gradually add milk mixture to flour mixture, beating at medium speed of a heavy-duty electric mixer. Turn dough out onto a lightly floured surface, and knead until smooth and elastic (about 10 minutes). Place dough in a well-greased bowl, turning to grease top. Cover and let rise in a warm place (85°), free from drafts, 1 hour or until doubled in bulk.

Punch dough down; turn out onto a lightly floured surface, and knead lightly 4 or 5 times. Sprinkle baking sheet with cornmeal. Divide dough into 12 (5- x 1-inch) loaf-shaped rolls; place on baking sheet. Cover and let rise in a warm place, free from drafts, 1 hour or until doubled in bulk. Score tops of rolls with a sharp knife, making ¼-inch-deep slashes.

Place a loafpan of boiling water on lower rack of oven. Place baking sheet on middle rack of oven, and bake at 450° for 15 minutes. Let rolls cool completely on wire racks. Yield: 1 dozen.

White Chocolate Mousse

1 egg
1 egg yolk
6 ounces white chocolate, coarsely chopped
1 cup whipping cream
1 teaspoon unflavored gelatin
1 tablespoon light rum
1 tablespoon white crème de cacao
Sprigs of fresh mint (optional)
Dark chocolate curls (optional)

Beat egg and egg yolk in a large bowl at high speed of an electric mixer until thick and lemon colored. Place white chocolate in top of a double boiler; bring water to a boil. Reduce heat to low; cook, stirring constantly, until chocolate melts. Gradually add one-fourth of melted chocolate to egg mixture; add to remaining hot mixture, stirring constantly. Cook 1 minute, stirring constantly. Pour mixture into large bowl. Set aside until cooled.

Beat 1 cup whipping cream at medium speed of electric mixer until soft peaks form. Set aside.

Sprinkle gelatin over rum and crème de cacao in a small saucepan; let stand 1 minute. Cook over low heat, stirring until gelatin dissolves. Gradually add gelatin mixture, a few drops at a time, to chocolate mixture, beating until smooth.

Gently fold half of white chocolate mixture into whipped cream; add to remaining white chocolate, gently folding until combined. Spoon mixture into individual dessert dishes; chill at least 3 hours or until serving time. If desired, garnish with mint sprigs and chocolate curls. Yield: 6 servings.

White Chocolate Mousse is a rich, melt-in-your-mouth dessert. It looks pretty garnished with sprigs of fresh mint and dark chocolate curls.

Dinner Under the Trees

A large lawn with big shade trees provides the perfect spot for a bit of old-fashioned croquet. Afterwards, settle back and enjoy Endive Boats with Radish Spread and a cool cup of Gazpacho. Then sample Smoked Salmon Steaks with Cucumber-Mustard Sauce, Marinated New Potatoes, and Zesty Broccoli Spears—all delicious served with a superb smoky-flavored white wine. End the day with two proven favorites—Peppermint Ice Cream and Double Chocolate Chip Cookies.

Dinner Under the Trees

Endive Boats with Radish Spread

Gazpacho

Smoked Salmon Steaks with
Cucumber-Mustard Sauce

Marinated New Potatoes

Zesty Broccoli Spears

Rosemount Estate Chardonnay-Show Reserve

Peppermint Ice Cream

Double Chocolate Chip Cookies

Coffee

Water

Serves eight

Endive Boats with Radish Spread

3 small heads Belgian endive
1 (8-ounce) container whipped
   cream cheese, softened
⅓ cup finely minced radishes
2 tablespoons minced fresh
   chives
1½ teaspoons lemon-pepper
   seasoning
Spicy alfalfa sprouts

Peel leaves from cores of endive. Wash leaves, and pat dry with paper towels. Place leaves in a plastic bag, and refrigerate.

Combine cream cheese, radishes, chives, and lemon-pepper seasoning; stir with a fork until blended. Spoon mixture into a decorating bag fitted with tip No. 18. Place 3 to 4 sprouts inside each endive leaf, with sprout leaves near endive leaf tip. Pipe about 1 tablespoon cheese mixture, zigzag fashion, down center of each endive leaf, covering stems of sprouts. Chill until ready to serve. Yield: about 2 dozen.

Gazpacho

3 cups tomato juice
2 cups peeled, chopped tomato
1 (10¾-ounce) can tomato soup, undiluted
1¼ cups water
¾ cup peeled, chopped cucumber
½ cup chopped green pepper
½ cup chopped onion
¼ cup commercial Italian salad dressing
2 tablespoons red wine vinegar
1 tablespoon lemon juice
¼ to ½ teaspoon hot sauce
¼ teaspoon salt
¼ teaspoon pepper
⅛ teaspoon garlic powder
Dash of white wine Worcestershire sauce
Cucumber slices

Combine all ingredients except cucumber slices; stir well. Cover and chill at least 8 hours. Ladle into large, stemmed glasses; garnish with cucumber slices. Yield: 9 cups.

Smoked Salmon Steaks with Cucumber-Mustard Sauce

8 (1- to 1½-inch-thick) salmon steaks (with skin on)
2 cups water
½ cup firmly packed brown sugar
1 tablespoon salt
1 teaspoon ground red pepper
Cucumber-Mustard Sauce
Sprigs of fresh chives (optional)

Place salmon steaks in two large shallow dishes. Combine next 4 ingredients; stir well. Pour marinade over fish. Cover and refrigerate 6 hours, turning fish occasionally.

Prepare charcoal fire in smoker, and let burn 10 to 15 minutes. Cover coals with large pieces of hickory. Place water pan in smoker, and fill with hot water.

Place salmon steaks on food rack in smoker. Cover with smoker lid, and cook 1 to 1½ hours or to desired degree of doneness, adding charcoal as needed. Remove steaks to serving plates. Serve salmon steaks with Cucumber-Mustard Sauce. Garnish with fresh chives, if desired. Yield: 8 servings.

Cucumber-Mustard Sauce

¾ cup sour cream
½ cup peeled, chopped cucumber
¼ cup mayonnaise
¼ cup prepared mustard
1 tablespoon chopped fresh chives
½ teaspoon chopped fresh parsley
¼ teaspoon salt
¼ teaspoon dried whole dillweed

Combine all ingredients, stirring well. Cover and chill at least 1 hour. Yield: 1¾ cups.

Smoked Salmon Steaks with Cucumber-Mustard Sauce, Marinated New Potatoes, and Zesty Broccoli Spears form a fine, tasty meal.

Marinated New Potatoes

2 pounds small new potatoes,
  unpeeled
2 (0.7-ounce) packages Italian
  salad dressing mix
¼ cup minced green onions
3 tablespoons minced fresh
  parsley
1 (2-ounce) jar diced pimiento,
  drained
Leaf lettuce

Cook potatoes in boiling water to cover 10 to 15 minutes or until tender; drain and let cool. Cut potatoes into ¼-inch slices; arrange in a shallow serving dish. Set aside.

Prepare salad dressing mix according to package directions; stir in green onions, parsley, and pimiento. Pour over potatoes; cover and chill. Spoon potatoes over lettuce leaves, using a slotted spoon. Yield: 8 servings.

Zesty Broccoli Spears

2 pounds fresh broccoli
1 cup orange juice
2 tablespoons grated orange rind
2 teaspoons lemon juice
¼ teaspoon garlic salt
⅛ teaspoon garlic powder
3 tablespoons white wine vinegar
2 tablespoons olive oil

Trim off large leaves of broccoli, and remove tough ends of lower stalks. Wash broccoli thoroughly, and cut into spears. Cook broccoli in a small amount of boiling water 10 to 12 minutes or just until tender. Drain; place broccoli in a serving dish.

Combine orange juice, orange rind, lemon juice, garlic salt, and garlic powder in a small saucepan; stir well. Cover and cook over medium-low heat 10 minutes. Remove from heat; stir in vinegar and oil with a wire whisk. Pour mixture over broccoli. Use a slotted spoon to serve. Yield: 8 servings.

Peppermint Ice Cream

4 cups milk
3 eggs
¾ cup sugar
2½ cups half-and-half
½ cup crushed hard peppermint
  candy
Additional crushed hard
  peppermint candy (optional)

Place milk in top of a large double boiler; bring water to a boil. Cook until milk is thoroughly heated. Remove from heat, and set aside.

Beat eggs at medium speed of an electric mixer until frothy. Add sugar, beating until thickened. Gradually stir about one-fourth of hot milk into egg mixture; add to remaining hot milk, stirring constantly. Cook custard mixture in top of double boiler over low heat, stirring frequently, until mixture begins to thicken and coats a metal spoon. Remove from heat; stir in half-and-half and ½ cup crushed candy. Cover and chill mixture several hours or until candy has dissolved.

Pour custard mixture into freezer can of a 1-gallon hand-turned or electric freezer. Freeze according to manufacturer's instructions. Let ripen at least 1 hour. Sprinkle each serving lightly with additional crushed peppermint candy, if desired. Yield: 2½ quarts.

Double Chocolate Chip Cookies

1 (6-ounce) package semisweet
  chocolate morsels, divided
1½ cups all-purpose flour
1 teaspoon baking powder
½ teaspoon salt
½ cup shortening
½ cup sugar
½ cup firmly packed brown sugar
1 egg
1 teaspoon vanilla extract
2 tablespoons milk
1 cup chopped pecans

Place ½ cup chocolate morsels in top of a double boiler; bring water to a boil. Reduce heat to low; cook until chocolate melts, stirring occasionally. Set aside to cool.

Combine flour, baking powder, and salt; set aside. Cream shortening; gradually add sugars, beating well at medium speed of an electric mixer. Add melted chocolate, egg, and vanilla; beat well. Stir in milk. Gradually add flour mixture, and mix well. Stir in remaining ½ cup chocolate morsels and pecans.

Drop dough by heaping teaspoonfuls onto lightly greased cookie sheets. Bake at 350° for 10 to 12 minutes or until done. Let cool slightly; carefully transfer cookies to wire racks to cool completely. Yield: about 6 dozen.

Guests will love Peppermint Ice Cream and Double Chocolate Chip Cookies. Be prepared to offer second helpings.

Grilled Outdoor Dinner

Celebrate a sunny summer day with this outdoor meal. Whet appetites with Jalapeño and Pimiento Squares and Marinated Garbanzo Bean Salad. Then offer Rosemary Grilled Chicken with Red Pepper Sauce, Vegetable Kabobs, and Individual Cornbread Loaves. Finish with big bowls of Honey-Lemon Ice Cream. The entire meal will go down easily with cool glasses of White Sangría.

Grilled Outdoor Dinner

Jalapeño and Pimiento Squares

Marinated Garbanzo Bean Salad

Rosemary Grilled Chicken with
Red Pepper Sauce

Vegetable Kabobs

Individual Cornbread Loaves

Honey-Lemon Ice Cream

White Sangría

Water

Serves six

Jalapeño and Pimiento Squares

4 cups (16 ounces) shredded
   Cheddar cheese
4 eggs, beaten
3 canned jalapeño peppers,
   seeded and chopped
1 (2-ounce) jar diced pimiento,
   drained
1 teaspoon minced onion

Combine all ingredients in a medium bowl; stir well. Spread mixture in a lightly greased 8-inch square baking pan. Bake at 350° for 30 to 40 minutes; let stand 10 minutes. Cut into squares, and serve immediately. Yield: 3 dozen.

Turn a hot afternoon into a party by offering Jalapeño and Pimiento Squares with a pitcher of White Sangría.

Marinated Garbanzo Bean Salad

½ pound dried garbanzo beans
  (1¼ cups)
1 (2-ounce) jar diced pimiento,
  drained
2 green onions, thinly sliced
1 tablespoon chopped fresh
  parsley
2 tablespoons sugar
¼ cup plus 2 tablespoons vinegar
2 tablespoons vegetable oil
2 tablespoons olive oil
¼ teaspoon salt
¼ teaspoon white pepper
Curly lettuce leaves
1½ cups coarsely shredded
  iceberg lettuce

Sort and wash beans; place in a Dutch oven. Cover with water 2 inches above beans; let soak overnight. Drain beans; return to Dutch oven, and cover with water. Cover and bring to a boil; reduce heat, and simmer 1 to 1½ hours or until beans are tender. Drain and let cool.

Combine beans, pimiento, green onions, and parsley in a medium bowl; stir gently. Combine sugar and next 5 ingredients in a small saucepan. Bring to a boil over medium heat, and cook, stirring occasionally, until sugar dissolves. Pour over bean mixture, tossing gently. Cover and chill at least 4 hours.

To serve, arrange curly lettuce leaves on individual salad plates. Top with shredded iceberg lettuce; arrange bean mixture over shredded lettuce. Yield: 6 servings.

Serve guests Rosemary Grilled Chicken with Red Pepper Sauce, Vegetable Kabobs, and Individual Cornbread Loaves.

Rosemary Grilled Chicken with Red Pepper Sauce

1 tablespoon Dijon mustard
1 tablespoon lemon juice
6 chicken breast halves, skinned
½ teaspoon coarsely ground
  pepper
¼ cup butter or margarine
¼ cup lemon juice
2 teaspoons dried whole
  rosemary, crushed
½ teaspoon garlic powder
Red Pepper Sauce

Combine mustard and 1 tablespoon lemon juice, stirring well. Spread mustard mixture on both sides of chicken, and sprinkle with pepper. Cover and chill 2 hours.

Melt butter in a small saucepan; stir in ¼ cup lemon juice, rosemary, and garlic powder. Cook over low heat 5 minutes, stirring occasionally.

Place chicken on grill over medium coals. Cover and grill 10 minutes on each side. Baste with butter mixture; grill an additional 10 to 15 minutes or until done, turning and basting frequently. Serve with Red Pepper Sauce. Yield: 6 servings.

Red Pepper Sauce

2 small sweet red peppers,
  chopped
1 large canned jalapeño pepper,
  seeded and chopped
1 tablespoon butter or margarine
¼ teaspoon garlic powder
3 medium tomatoes (1½ pounds),
  peeled, seeded, and chopped
¼ teaspoon salt
¼ teaspoon pepper

Combine first 4 ingredients in a saucepan. Cook over medium heat 4 minutes or until red pepper is tender. Add tomato; cook 5 minutes, stirring occasionally. Add salt and pepper. Transfer tomato mixture to container of an electric blender; top with cover, and process until smooth. Return puree to saucepan. Cook over medium heat until slightly thickened, stirring frequently. Yield: 1½ cups.

Vegetable Kabobs

12 boiling onions, peeled
3 medium ears fresh corn
3 medium zucchini
¾ cup butter or margarine,
   melted
3 tablespoons minced fresh
   chives
½ teaspoon seasoned salt

Cook onions in boiling water to cover 5 minutes; drain and set aside.

Remove shucks and silks from corn. Slice corn and zucchini into 1-inch pieces, using an electric knife, if desired. Alternate vegetables on 6 large metal skewers, placing 2 pieces corn, 3 pieces zucchini, and 2 onions on each skewer.

Combine butter, chives, and salt, stirring well. Place kabobs on grill over medium coals; grill 10 minutes or until zucchini is tender, turning and basting with butter mixture every 2 minutes. Yield: 6 servings.

Individual Cornbread Loaves

¾ cup yellow cornmeal
¾ cup all-purpose flour
3 tablespoons sugar
2 teaspoons baking powder
1 teaspoon baking soda
¾ teaspoon seasoned salt
1 egg, beaten
1 (8-ounce) carton sour cream
3 tablespoons milk
3 tablespoons shortening, melted

Combine first 6 ingredients in a large bowl; make a well in center of mixture. Combine egg, sour cream, milk, and shortening; add to dry ingredients, stirring just until moistened. Spoon into 6 greased 4- x 2- x 2-inch loafpans; bake at 425° for 15 minutes or until lightly browned. Remove from pans immediately. Yield: six (4- x 2- x 2-inch) loaves.

Honey-Lemon Ice Cream

4½ cups milk
1 cup sugar
¼ cup plus 2 tablespoons
   all-purpose flour
½ teaspoon salt
½ cup honey
5 eggs, beaten
1 quart whipping cream
1 tablespoon lemon extract
1 teaspoon vanilla extract

Place milk in a 3-quart saucepan over low heat; cook until thoroughly heated, but not boiling. Combine sugar, flour, and salt; gradually add sugar mixture to milk, stirring until blended. Stir in honey. Cook over medium heat 15 to 20 minutes or until thickened, stirring constantly.

Stir one-fourth of hot mixture into beaten eggs; add to remaining hot mixture, stirring constantly. Cook 1 minute; remove from heat, and cool 15 minutes. Chill custard mixture at least 2 hours.

Combine whipping cream and flavorings in a large bowl; add chilled custard, stirring with a wire whisk. Pour mixture into freezer can of a 1-gallon hand-turned or electric freezer. Freeze according to manufacturer's instructions. Let ripen at least 2 hours before serving. Yield: 3 quarts.

White Sangría

1 (750-milliliter) bottle Chablis or
   other dry white wine
2 lemons, sliced
1 orange, sliced
2 tablespoons powdered sugar
2 tablespoons kirsch or other
   cherry-flavored brandy
3 tablespoons Cointreau or other
   orange-flavored liqueur
1½ cups club soda, chilled
Sprigs of fresh mint

Pour wine into a large pitcher. Add lemon and orange slices, sugar, kirsch, and Cointreau, stirring well. Cover and refrigerate at least 6 to 8 hours. Stir in club soda just before serving. Serve over ice. Garnish with mint. Yield: 6 cups.

Dinner in the Gazebo

The best time to enjoy a garden is in the spring when it is in full bloom. This is also the time to relish Caponata with Italian Pita Triangles and a light, dry red wine. A cool, shaded gazebo is the perfect place to offer Sugar Snap Soup, Tomato-Basil Salad, Angel Hair Pasta with Lobster Sauce, and a glass of zesty, earthy-flavored chardonnay. But make sure everyone saves room for a slice of Chocolate Pecan Pie with Orange Cream; it's the ultimate in thick, rich pies.

109

Dinner in the Gazebo

Caponata with Italian Pita Triangles

Dolcetto D'Alba-Ceretto

Sugar Snap Soup

Tomato-Basil Salad

Angel Hair Pasta with Lobster Sauce

Louis Jadot Pouilly-Fuissé

Chocolate Pecan Pie with
Orange Cream

Coffee

Water

Serves four

Caponata with Italian Pita Triangles

1 (1-pound) eggplant
1 tablespoon plus 1 teaspoon
  olive oil
1 cup minced green onions
1 cup minced celery
1 medium-size sweet red pepper,
  minced
2 cloves garlic, minced
1 (8-ounce) can tomato sauce
¼ cup plus 2 tablespoons salad
  olives
3 tablespoons tomato paste
2 tablespoons red wine vinegar
1 tablespoon sugar
¼ teaspoon pepper
¼ teaspoon dried whole oregano
Sprigs of fresh basil
Sprigs of fresh parsley
Italian Pita Triangles

Cut eggplant in half lengthwise. Scoop out pulp, and dice (about 4 cups). Reserve shells to serve dip in, if desired.

Place oil in a large nonaluminum Dutch oven over medium heat. Add diced eggplant, green onions, celery, red pepper, and garlic. Cook 10 minutes, stirring frequently. Add tomato sauce and next 6 ingredients, stirring well. Cook over low heat, stirring frequently, 25 minutes or until vegetables are tender. Transfer to a medium bowl. Cover and chill 8 hours. Spoon into eggplant shells, if desired. Garnish with basil and parsley. Serve with Italian Pita Triangles. Yield: 3⅓ cups.

Caponata, a zesty eggplant dip, teams perfectly with Italian Pita Triangles and a glass of dry red wine.

Sugar Snap Soup

Italian Pita Triangles

2 (6-inch) pita bread rounds
3 tablespoons sesame oil
½ teaspoon dried whole oregano
¼ teaspoon garlic powder

Separate each pita bread into 2 rounds by cutting along outer edges; cut each into 6 wedges to make 24 triangles. Place wedges, rough side up, on an ungreased baking sheet.

Combine oil, oregano, and garlic powder, stirring well. Lightly brush rough surface of wedges with oil mixture. Bake at 325° for 10 minutes or until wedges are dry and golden. Yield: 2 dozen.

1 pound fresh Sugar Snap peas
3½ cups canned chicken broth, undiluted
½ cup shredded lettuce
½ cup chopped onion
2 cups half-and-half
1 bay leaf

1 teaspoon salt
¼ teaspoon white pepper
⅛ teaspoon freshly grated nutmeg
1 egg yolk
2 teaspoons butter or margarine
2 teaspoons minced fresh parsley

Trim ends and stems from pea pods. Combine pea pods, broth, lettuce, and onion in a large saucepan. Bring mixture to a boil. Cover, reduce heat, and simmer 20 minutes or until peas are tender. Pour mixture into container of an electric blender; top with cover, and process until pureed. Return puree to saucepan; stir in half-and-half, bay leaf, salt, pepper, and nutmeg. Cook over low heat, stirring constantly, until mixture is thoroughly heated.

Beat egg yolk until thick and lemon colored. Gradually stir about 2 tablespoons hot mixture into yolk; add to remaining hot mixture, stirring constantly. Cook over low heat, stirring constantly, just until soup is bubbly. Remove and discard bay leaf. Stir in butter and parsley. Serve warm. Yield: about 5 cups.

Angel Hair Pasta with Lobster Sauce, laced with white wine and mushrooms, is a variation of lobster thermidor.

Tomato-Basil Salad

3 large tomatoes
2 green onions, chopped
¼ cup olive oil
3 tablespoons red wine vinegar
1 tablespoon minced fresh basil
½ teaspoon salt
½ teaspoon dried Italian
  seasoning
¼ teaspoon powdered
  sugar
¼ teaspoon coarsely ground
  pepper
⅛ teaspoon garlic salt
Bibb lettuce leaves
Sprigs of fresh basil

Cut each tomato into 8 wedges. Place wedges in a shallow container; sprinkle with onions. Combine oil and next 7 ingredients, stirring well. Pour over tomatoes. Cover and marinate in refrigerator 1 hour. Arrange lettuce on salad plates; top with tomato mixture. Garnish with basil. Yield: 4 servings.

Angel Hair Pasta with Lobster Sauce

2 quarts water
2 (10-ounce) lobster tails, fresh
  or frozen, thawed
½ (16-ounce) package angel hair
  pasta
⅔ cup sliced fresh mushrooms
3 tablespoons chopped green
  onions
2 tablespoons butter or
  margarine, melted
2 tablespoons all-purpose flour
1 cup plus 2 tablespoons
  half-and-half
2 tablespoons Chablis or other
  dry white wine
2 tablespoons chopped
  pimiento
¼ teaspoon salt
¼ teaspoon dry mustard
Dash of red pepper
Paprika
2 tablespoons freshly grated
  Parmesan cheese
Sprigs of fresh parsley

Bring water to a boil; add lobster tails. Cover, reduce heat, and simmer 6 minutes. Drain; rinse with cold water. Drain again. Split and clean tails. Cut meat into ½-inch pieces. Cook pasta according to package directions. Drain.

Sauté mushrooms and onions in butter until tender. Add flour, stirring until smooth. Cook 1 minute, stirring constantly. Gradually add half-and-half; cook over medium heat, stirring constantly, until thickened and bubbly. Stir in wine, pimiento, salt, mustard, red pepper, and lobster meat. Cook over low heat, stirring constantly, until thoroughly heated. Serve sauce over pasta. Sprinkle with paprika and cheese, and garnish with parsley. Yield: 4 servings.

Chocolate Pecan Pie with Orange Cream

½ cup chopped pecans
1 tablespoon bourbon
3 eggs, beaten
1 cup sugar
¾ cup light corn syrup
¼ cup butter or margarine,
  melted
½ teaspoon vanilla extract
½ teaspoon orange extract
¼ teaspoon salt
½ cup semisweet chocolate
  morsels
1 unbaked 9-inch pastry shell
Orange Cream

Combine pecans and bourbon; set aside. Combine eggs and next 6 ingredients; mix well. Stir in chocolate morsels and pecan mixture; pour into pastry shell. Bake at 350° for 50 minutes or until set. Let cool. Top each slice with a dollop of Orange Cream. Yield: one 9-inch pie.

Orange Cream

1 (3-ounce) package cream
  cheese, softened
½ (7-ounce) jar marshmallow
  cream
1 teaspoon grated orange rind
2 teaspoons frozen orange juice
  concentrate, thawed

Combine cream cheese and marshmallow cream; beat until smooth. Stir in orange rind and orange juice concentrate. Cover and chill 1 hour. Yield: about 1 cup.

Silver Anniversary Dinner

Twenty-five years marks a special anniversary to share with close friends. Create a spectacular setting by polishing your best silver and hanging a fabulous bouquet from an overhead fixture. Begin the dinner with Shrimp Cocktail with Mustard-Horseradish Sauce. Then follow with Sugared Almond Salad with Orange Vinaigrette, Grouper in Pecan Butter, Sautéed Peppers, Salt-Roasted Potatoes, and a rich, buttery-flavored white wine. An elegant dessert of Ruby Berries and Cream will complete this lovely meal.

Silver Anniversary Dinner

Shrimp Cocktail with
Mustard-Horseradish Sauce

Sugared Almond Salad with
Orange Vinaigrette

Grouper in Pecan Butter

Sautéed Peppers

Salt-Roasted Potatoes

Jordan Chardonnay

Ruby Berries and Cream

Coffee

Water

Serves six

Shrimp Cocktail with Mustard-Horseradish Sauce

4 quarts water
1 small onion, sliced
1 lemon, sliced
1 (1½-ounce) package prepared
  shrimp boil
2 tablespoons salt
1 clove garlic, sliced
2 pounds unpeeled large fresh
  shrimp (about 3 dozen)
1½ cups finely shredded lettuce
Mustard-Horseradish Sauce

Combine first 6 ingredients in a
Dutch oven; bring to a boil. Add
shrimp, and cook 3 to 5 minutes.
Drain; rinse with cold water. Peel
shrimp, leaving tails intact. Chill.
Divide shredded lettuce evenly
among 6 stemmed cocktail glasses;

top each bed of lettuce with a large dollop of Mustard-Horseradish Sauce. Divide chilled shrimp evenly among glasses, arranging with tails extended over edge of each glass. Serve immediately. Yield: 6 appetizer servings.

Mustard-Horseradish Sauce

1 (8-ounce) carton sour cream
¼ cup plus 2 tablespoons mayonnaise
¼ cup Dijon mustard
1 tablespoon plus 1 teaspoon prepared horseradish
1 tablespoon grated onion
1 tablespoon lemon juice
1 teaspoon garlic powder
½ teaspoon ground red pepper

Combine all ingredients in a small bowl; stir well. Cover and chill thoroughly. Yield: 1⅔ cups.

Sugared Almond Salad with Orange Vinaigrette

1 egg white
¼ cup sugar
1 cup sliced almonds
2 tablespoons butter or margarine, melted
1 head Bibb lettuce, torn into bite-size pieces
1 head leaf lettuce, torn into bite-size pieces
1 (11-ounce) can mandarin oranges, drained
10 fresh strawberries, thinly sliced
1 green onion, chopped
¾ cup olive oil
¼ cup red wine vinegar
1 tablespoon orange juice
1 teaspoon grated orange rind
½ teaspoon poppyseeds
⅛ teaspoon salt
⅛ teaspoon pepper

Beat egg white (at room temperature) at high speed of an electric mixer until foamy. Gradually add sugar, 1 tablespoon at a time, beating until stiff peaks form. Fold in almonds. Pour butter into a 9-inch square baking pan. Spread coated almonds in pan over butter. Bake at 325° for 20 to 25 minutes or until almonds are dry, stirring every 5 minutes. Set aside to let almonds cool completely.

Combine lettuce, oranges, strawberries, and green onion; toss gently. Combine olive oil and remaining ingredients; beat with a wire whisk until blended. Pour over salad, tossing gently. Arrange salad on individual salad plates. Sprinkle each with sugared almonds. Yield: 6 servings.

Sugared Almond Salad with Orange Vinaigrette features an intriguing combination of flavors. Sweet oranges, strawberries, and crisp sugared almonds help balance the tangy vinaigrette dressing.

Grouper in Pecan Butter

⅓ cup butter
½ cup chopped pecans, toasted
1 tablespoon brown sugar
¼ teaspoon garlic powder
1 teaspoon lemon juice
2 dashes of hot sauce
½ cup milk
1 egg, beaten
2 teaspoons salt
1 teaspoon onion powder
¾ teaspoon paprika
½ teaspoon garlic powder
½ teaspoon white pepper
½ teaspoon ground red pepper
¼ teaspoon dry mustard
6 (6-ounce) grouper fillets
1½ cups all-purpose flour
Vegetable oil
¼ cup plus 2 tablespoons
  chopped pecans, toasted

Combine first 6 ingredients in container of an electric blender or food processor; top with cover, and process until smooth. Transfer butter mixture to a small bowl; chill.

Combine milk and egg in a large shallow container, stirring well; set aside. Combine salt, onion powder, paprika, garlic powder, white pepper, red pepper, and dry mustard in a small bowl, stirring well; set aside.

Sprinkle fillets generously with salt mixture; dredge in flour. Dip each fillet in egg mixture; dredge again in flour. Fry fillets in hot oil (350°) for 2 to 3 minutes on each side or until browned. Drain on paper towels.

Place fillets on a warm serving platter; top each with a dollop of butter mixture. Sprinkle with toasted pecans. Yield: 6 servings.

Sautéed Peppers

1 medium-size sweet yellow
  pepper, cut into thin strips
2 medium-size sweet red peppers,
  cut into thin strips
2 medium-size green peppers, cut
  into thin strips
2 tablespoons olive oil
½ teaspoon dried whole basil
¼ teaspoon salt

Sauté pepper strips in oil until crisp-tender. Sprinkle with basil and salt; serve immediately. Yield: 6 servings.

Salt-Roasted Potatoes

18 small new potatoes, unpeeled
2 tablespoons vegetable oil
2 teaspoons kosher salt

Scrub potatoes. Place in a 13- x 9- x 2-inch baking dish. Bake at 450° for 20 minutes, turning potatoes after 10 minutes. Brush potatoes with oil, turning to coat. Sprinkle potatoes on all sides with salt. Bake an additional 10 minutes or until potatoes are tender. Yield: 6 servings.

Ruby Berries and Cream

2 (10-ounce) packages frozen
  raspberries, thawed
1 cup sifted powdered sugar,
  divided
2 tablespoons Cointreau or other
  orange-flavored liqueur
1 tablespoon orange juice
6 cups fresh strawberries, hulled
Whipped cream

Press raspberries through a sieve to remove seeds; discard seeds. Combine raspberry puree, ½ cup powdered sugar, Cointreau, and orange juice; stir well.

Combine strawberries and remaining ½ cup powdered sugar; toss gently. Pour raspberry sauce over strawberries; cover and chill 3 hours. Spoon strawberry mixture evenly into 6 dessert dishes. Top each with a dollop of whipped cream. Yield: 6 servings.

Serve a meal worthy of a silver celebration when you offer Grouper in Pecan Butter, Sautéed Peppers, and Salt-Roasted Potatoes.

Dinner in the Arbor

The lacy lavender of a wisteria arbor surrounds this inviting dinner. A glass of crisp champagne is wonderful served with Champagne Pâté. The menu of Greek Salad, Veal Piccata, Fettuccine Alfredo, and Marinated Asparagus is matched with a tart, velvety, sweet red wine. Baklava, Strawberries and Crema, and a sparkling wine round out the meal.

Dinner in the Arbor

Champagne Pâté

Laurent-Perrier Brut

Greek Salad

Veal Piccata

Fettuccine Alfredo

Marinated Asparagus

Brunello di Montalcino

Baklava

Strawberries and Crema

Schramsberg Crémant

Coffee

Serves four

Champagne Pâté

2 tablespoons minced green onions
1 pound chicken livers
2 tablespoons butter, melted
⅓ cup champagne
¼ cup whipping cream
½ teaspoon salt
⅛ teaspoon garlic powder
⅛ teaspoon ground allspice
⅛ teaspoon ground nutmeg
⅛ teaspoon ground red pepper
½ cup butter, melted

Sauté green onions and livers in 2 tablespoons butter 6 to 8 minutes or until livers are slightly pink; spoon liver mixture into container of an electric blender or food processor.

Place champagne in a small saucepan; simmer over medium-low heat until reduced to 3 tablespoons. Add champagne, whipping cream, and next 5 ingredients to liver mixture. Top with cover, and process until smooth. Add ½ cup butter, and process until well blended.

Spoon liver mixture into a small crock. Chill several hours. Serve pâté with assorted fresh vegetables and crackers. Yield: 2 cups.

Veal Piccata, Fettuccine Alfredo, and Marinated Asparagus form a satisfying combination.

Greek Salad

1 clove garlic
1 small head Boston lettuce, torn
1 small head romaine lettuce, torn
⅔ cup crumbled feta cheese
5 ripe olives, sliced
3 green onions, sliced
2 radishes, sliced
1 stalk celery, chopped
½ medium cucumber, sliced
¼ cup olive oil
Juice of 1 lemon
2 teaspoons minced fresh parsley
½ teaspoon coarsely ground pepper
¼ teaspoon salt
¼ teaspoon dried whole oregano
2 small tomatoes, cut into wedges
1 small green pepper, cut into rings
4 anchovy fillets (optional)

Rub a large wooden salad bowl with garlic; discard garlic. Combine Boston lettuce and next 7 ingredients in salad bowl, tossing gently.

Combine olive oil and lemon juice in a small bowl; beat with a wire whisk. Pour over salad. Sprinkle with parsley, pepper, salt, and oregano. Gently toss salad. Top with tomatoes, green pepper, and, if desired, anchovies. Serve on individual salad plates. Yield: 4 servings.

Veal Piccata

1 pound veal cutlets
⅔ cup all-purpose flour
1 teaspoon salt
½ teaspoon garlic powder
½ teaspoon pepper
3 tablespoons butter
2 tablespoons olive oil
3 tablespoons lemon juice
3 tablespoons Chablis or other dry white wine
1 tablespoon chopped fresh parsley

Place veal between 2 sheets of wax paper; flatten to ¼-inch thickness, using a meat mallet or rolling pin. Cut veal into 8 serving-size pieces. Combine flour, salt, garlic powder, and pepper in a small bowl; stir well. Dredge veal in flour mixture.

Heat butter and oil in a large skillet over medium heat. Add veal, and cook 1 minute on each side. Remove meat to a heated platter, and keep warm. Drain off drippings. Add lemon juice and wine to skillet; cook over medium heat until thoroughly heated. To serve, spoon juice mixture over veal; sprinkle with parsley. Yield: 4 servings.

Fettuccine Alfredo

½ (16-ounce) package fettuccine
⅔ cup freshly grated Parmesan
   cheese
⅓ cup butter or margarine,
   softened
⅓ cup whipping cream
½ teaspoon coarsely ground
   pepper

Cook fettuccine according to package directions, omitting salt; drain. Transfer to a large bowl. Add remaining ingredients, tossing gently until butter melts and fettuccine is coated. Yield: 4 servings.

Marinated Asparagus

1 pound fresh asparagus
   spears
1 green onion, finely chopped
¼ cup commercial Italian salad
   dressing
2 tablespoons vinegar
2 tablespoons diced pimiento
1 tablespoon vegetable oil
¼ teaspoon salt
¼ teaspoon white pepper

Snap off tough ends of asparagus. Remove scales from stalks with a knife or vegetable peeler, if desired. Cook asparagus, covered, in a small amount of boiling water 5 to 6 minutes or until crisp-tender; drain. Rinse with cold water; drain again.

Place asparagus in a shallow serving dish. Combine green onion and remaining ingredients; stir well, and pour over asparagus. Cover and chill 3 hours; serve with a slotted spoon. Yield: 4 servings.

Baklava

1 (1-pound) package commercial
   frozen phyllo pastry, thawed
1¼ cups butter, melted
1 cup ground pecans
½ cup ground almonds
2 tablespoons brown sugar
1½ teaspoons ground cinnamon
¼ teaspoon ground nutmeg
½ cup sugar
½ cup water
¼ cup honey
1 tablespoon lemon juice

Cut phyllo in half crosswise; cut each half to fit a 13- x 9- x 2-inch baking pan. Layer 15 sheets of phyllo in a greased 13- x 9- x 2-inch baking pan, brushing each sheet with melted butter (keep remaining phyllo covered with a damp towel). Set remaining butter aside.

Combine pecans and next 4 ingredients, stirring well. Sprinkle half of nut mixture over phyllo in baking pan. Drizzle with a little melted butter. Top nut mixture with 15 additional sheets of phyllo, brushing each sheet with melted butter. Top phyllo with remaining nut mixture, and drizzle with a little melted butter. Top with remaining phyllo, brushing each sheet with melted butter. Using a sharp knife, score top of phyllo in a diamond design. Bake at 350° for 45 minutes or until golden. Let cool completely.

Combine ½ cup sugar, water, and honey in a saucepan. Bring to a boil; boil 10 minutes, stirring occasionally. Stir in lemon juice. Drizzle honey mixture over phyllo. Cut phyllo along scored lines. Let stand at room temperature 8 hours before serving. Yield: 3 dozen.

Strawberries and Crema

1 egg
2 tablespoons sugar
2¼ teaspoons all-purpose flour
⅛ teaspoon salt
1 cup milk
¼ teaspoon vanilla extract
2 cups strawberry halves

Beat egg in top of a double boiler until frothy. Combine sugar, flour, and salt; gradually add to egg, beating until thick. Place milk in a saucepan; cook over low heat until thoroughly heated. (Do not boil.) Gradually stir about one-fourth of hot milk into egg mixture; add remaining milk, stirring constantly. Bring water to a boil. Reduce heat to low; cook 10 to 20 minutes or until mixture thickens and coats a metal spoon. Stir in vanilla. Pour custard into a bowl and chill.

To serve, place ½ cup strawberries in each of 4 stemmed glasses. Drizzle ¼ cup chilled custard over each serving. Yield: 4 servings.

Guests will find Baklava and Strawberries and Crema irresistible.

Southern Vegetable Dinner

In the South, summer means vegetables—lots of vegetables. In fact, you could plan an entire menu around nature's bounty by offering Crisp-Fried Okra Appetizer, Cream of Corn Soup, Green Beans Amandine, Salsa Tomatoes, Lemony New Potatoes, and Confetti Cornbread. And for dessert, what else but Zucchini Cake. Spicy Mississippi River Tea is sure to be a hit; add orange slices and sprigs of fresh mint to make it look cool and refreshing.

Southern Vegetable Dinner

Crisp-Fried Okra Appetizer

Cream of Corn Soup

Green Beans Amandine

Salsa Tomatoes

Lemony New Potatoes

Confetti Cornbread

Zucchini Cake

Mississippi River Tea

Serves four

Crisp-Fried Okra Appetizer

1 pound fresh okra
2 eggs, beaten
3 to 5 drops hot sauce
1 cup yellow cornmeal
½ teaspoon salt
1 to 1¼ teaspoons ground
   red pepper
Vegetable oil

Wash okra; drain well. Cut off tips and stem ends and discard; cut okra into ½-inch slices.

Combine eggs and hot sauce in a large bowl; add okra, and toss to coat. Combine cornmeal, salt, and red pepper, stirring well. Dredge okra in cornmeal mixture.

Deep-fry okra in hot oil (375°) for 5 minutes or until browned. Drain on paper towels. Serve immediately. Yield: 4 servings.

Cream of Corn Soup

3 medium ears fresh corn
1 small onion, chopped
2 tablespoons butter or
  margarine, melted
1 bay leaf
Pinch of dried whole rosemary
Pinch of dried whole thyme
3 cups chicken broth
Pinch of dried whole basil
Dash of pepper
2 tablespoons diced pimiento,
  drained
½ cup whipping cream
Sprigs of fresh rosemary
  (optional)

Cut corn from cob, scraping cob to remove pulp. Set aside. Sauté onion in butter in a large saucepan over medium heat until tender. Add 1 cup corn, and cook 3 minutes.

Tie bay leaf, dried whole rosemary, and thyme in a cheesecloth bag. Add spice bag, broth, basil, and pepper to sautéed mixture, stirring well. Reduce heat, and simmer, uncovered, 45 minutes.

Remove and discard spice bag. Place corn mixture in container of an electric blender; top with cover, and process until smooth. Return mixture to skillet. Stir in pimiento and remaining corn. Bring to a boil; reduce heat, and simmer, uncovered, 20 minutes. Stir in whipping cream. Cook over low heat until thoroughly heated. Garnish with fresh rosemary, if desired. Yield: 4 cups.

Green Beans Amandine

1 pound fresh green beans
1 small ham hock
½ cup water
⅓ cup slivered blanched almonds
2 tablespoons minced onion
1 tablespoon butter or margarine,
  melted
¼ to ½ teaspoon salt

Wash beans, and remove strings. Cut beans into 1½-inch pieces. Place in a large saucepan; add ham hock and water. Bring to a boil; cover, reduce heat, and simmer 1 hour. Drain off excess liquid, discarding ham hock.

Sauté almonds and onion in butter until onion is tender; add to beans. Sprinkle with salt; toss lightly before serving. Yield: 4 servings.

Salsa Tomatoes

¾ cup vegetable oil
¾ cup vinegar
3 tablespoons sugar
1 teaspoon minced fresh cilantro
¼ teaspoon dried whole oregano
⅛ teaspoon salt
⅛ teaspoon celery seeds
⅛ teaspoon pepper
6 small tomatoes, unpeeled and
  cubed
4 green onions, finely chopped
1 (4-ounce) can chopped green
  chiles, drained
1 clove garlic, minced
Sprig of fresh basil

Combine first 8 ingredients in a jar; cover tightly, and shake vigorously. Pour over tomato and green onions; stir in chiles and garlic. Cover and marinate in refrigerator at least 2 hours. Garnish with basil; serve with a slotted spoon. Yield: 4 servings.

Lemony New Potatoes

1¼ pounds small new potatoes,
  unpeeled and quartered
1 tablespoon chopped fresh chives
1 tablespoon lemon juice
1 tablespoon butter or margarine,
  melted
1 teaspoon grated lemon rind
⅛ teaspoon hot sauce

Cook potatoes, covered, in boiling water to cover 8 minutes or just until tender. Drain. Combine chives and remaining ingredients, stirring well; pour over potatoes, tossing gently. Serve immediately. Yield: 4 servings.

Serve Crisp-Fried Okra Appetizer to the side of a bowl of Cream of Corn Soup.

Confetti Cornbread

1 cup buttermilk
2 eggs, beaten
2 cups self-rising cornmeal
2 tablespoons sugar
⅓ cup vegetable oil
½ cup chopped green pepper
½ cup chopped sweet
    red pepper

Combine buttermilk and eggs in a large bowl; stir in cornmeal and sugar. Add oil and peppers, stirring just until blended. Pour mixture into a greased 8½- x 4½- x 3-inch loafpan. Bake at 350° for 45 to 50 minutes. Yield: 1 loaf.

Zucchini Cake

½ cup butter or margarine,
    softened
1¾ cups sugar
2 (1-ounce) squares unsweetened
    chocolate, melted and cooled
3 eggs
½ cup half-and-half
1 teaspoon grated lemon rind
1 teaspoon vanilla extract
1¾ cups coarsely grated
    unpeeled zucchini
2½ cups all-purpose flour
2½ teaspoons baking powder
1 teaspoon baking soda
½ teaspoon salt
½ teaspoon ground cinnamon
½ teaspoon ground nutmeg
½ cup semisweet chocolate
    mini-morsels
1 tablespoon powdered sugar

Cream butter; gradually add 1¾ cups sugar, beating well at medium speed of an electric mixer. Beat in melted chocolate. Add eggs, one at a time, beating well after each addition. Beat in half-and-half, lemon rind, and vanilla. Stir in zucchini.

Combine flour and next 6 ingredients, tossing well. Add to creamed mixture, stirring well. Pour batter into a greased and floured 10-inch Bundt pan. Bake at 350° for 1 hour or until a wooden pick inserted in center of cake comes out clean. Cool cake in pan 10 minutes; remove from pan, and place on a wire rack to cool completely. Sift powdered sugar over cake. Yield: one 10-inch cake.

Mississippi River Tea

3 (3-inch) sticks cinnamon,
    broken into pieces
¾ teaspoon whole cloves
½ teaspoon whole allspice
4 cups hot brewed tea
⅓ cup sugar
3 cups orange juice
1 cup unsweetened pineapple
    juice
Orange slices (optional)
Sprigs of fresh mint (optional)

Combine cinnamon, cloves, and allspice in a tea ball or cheesecloth bag, and set aside.

Combine hot tea and sugar in a large Dutch oven; stir in fruit juices. Add spice bag, and bring to a boil. Cover, reduce heat, and simmer 30 minutes; remove and discard spice bag. Serve tea over ice. If desired, garnish with orange slices and mint sprigs. Yield: 8 cups.

Chocolate-flavored Zucchini Cake is a tasty surprise. It looks pretty garnished with edible flowers.

Supper on the Porch

A screened porch provides a perfect place for entertaining intimate groups of guests. Start by offering Thick and Rich Piña Coladas, Caviar Mousse, and a sparkling white wine. When the sun sets, candlelight adds even more sparkle to this menu of Tabbouleh Salad, Grilled Tuna with Red Pepper Butter, Wild Rice with Pecans, Summer Squash Stir-Fry, and a sweet red wine. Large squares of gingerbread are delicious for dessert, especially when topped with raspberries and whipped cream.

Supper on the Porch

Thick and Rich Piña Coladas

Caviar Mousse

Château St. Jean Brut Blanc de Blancs

———

Tabbouleh Salad

Grilled Tuna with Red Pepper Butter

Wild Rice with Pecans

Summer Squash Stir-Fry

Acacia Pinot Noir

———

Gingerbread with Raspberries
and Cream

Coffee

Serves twelve

Thick and Rich Piña Coladas

3 (8½-ounce) cans cream of coconut
3 (8-ounce) cans crushed pineapple, undrained
3 cups vanilla ice cream
1 cup flaked coconut
¾ cup light rum
3 tablespoons crème de bananes
9 cups crushed ice
Additional flaked coconut

Combine 1 can cream of coconut, 1 can pineapple, 1 cup ice cream, ⅓ cup coconut, ¼ cup rum, and 1 tablespoon crème de bananes in container of an electric blender; top with cover, and process until smooth. Gradually add 3 cups crushed ice, processing until mixture is smooth and thickened. Pour into stemmed glasses, and sprinkle with additional coconut. Repeat procedure two times with remaining ingredients. Yield: 15 cups.

If you yearn for something cold and sweet to drink, then take a sip of Thick and Rich Piña Coladas.

Caviar Mousse

2 packages unflavored gelatin
½ cup lemon juice
1½ teaspoons white wine
    Worcestershire sauce
¾ teaspoon hot sauce
12 hard-cooked eggs, sieved
2¼ cups mayonnaise
3 (2-ounce) jars red caviar,
    drained

Lightly oil a 5½-cup mold; place in freezer for 30 minutes. Combine first 4 ingredients in top of a double boiler. Bring water to a boil; reduce heat to low, and cook until gelatin dissolves. Remove from heat; add eggs and mayonnaise, stirring well. Spoon about three-fourths of egg mixture into prepared mold, spreading to fill sides of mold and leaving a

well through center of mixture. Freeze 10 minutes.

Combine remaining one-fourth of egg mixture and caviar; stir well. Remove mold from freezer; pour caviar mixture into well. Chill 8 hours. Unmold and serve with crackers. Yield: 5½ cups.

Tabbouleh Salad

½ cup bulgur wheat
1 cup boiling water
1 large bunch fresh parsley
1 medium head iceberg lettuce
2 large tomatoes, diced
1 bunch green onions, finely
    chopped
Juice of 2 large lemons (½ cup)
2 tablespoons olive oil
1 teaspoon salt
¾ teaspoon pepper
¼ teaspoon dried mint flakes
Radicchio leaves (optional)

Place bulgur in a medium bowl. Add boiling water. Cover and let stand 1 hour. Drain off excess water, if necessary.

Rinse parsley and lettuce in cold water; drain and pat dry with paper towels. Chop parsley and shred lettuce. Combine parsley, lettuce, tomato, green onions, and bulgur. Combine lemon juice and next 4 ingredients; stir with a wire whisk until blended. Pour over salad; toss gently. Garnish with radicchio leaves, if desired. Serve immediately. Yield: 12 servings.

Grilled Tuna with Red Pepper Butter

3 (7-ounce) jars roasted red
    peppers, well drained
1½ cups butter, softened
1 teaspoon dried whole basil
½ teaspoon ground red pepper
¼ teaspoon dry mustard
12 (¾-inch-thick) tuna steaks
    (about 5 to 6 pounds)
1 tablespoon coarsely ground
    pepper
Sprigs of fresh basil (optional)

Position knife blade in food processor bowl; add roasted peppers. Top with cover, and process until pureed. Add butter, 1 tablespoon at a time, blending well after each addition. Add 1 teaspoon basil, ground red pepper, and mustard; blend well. Place 1 cup butter mixture on wax paper; shape into a log 2 inches in diameter. Cover and chill 8 hours. Cover remaining butter mixture, and chill 8 hours.

Place steaks on a grill over hot coals. Grill 4 minutes on each side or until fish flakes easily when tested with a fork, basting steaks with about ¼ cup reserved butter mixture. Remove steaks from grill; sprinkle with pepper. Garnish with fresh basil, if desired. Serve steaks with slices of butter log. Yield: 12 servings.

Wild Rice with Pecans

2 tablespoons butter or margarine
2 (6-ounce) packages long-grain
  and wild rice mix
4 cups chicken broth
8 green onions, chopped
8 medium mushrooms, sliced
1½ cups chopped pecans, toasted

Melt butter in a large Dutch oven. Add rice; cook over medium heat until lightly browned, stirring frequently. Stir in rice mix seasoning packets, broth, green onions, and mushrooms. Bring to a boil. Remove from heat. Pour into a lightly greased 3-quart casserole. Cover and bake at 350° for 30 minutes. Remove cover, and bake an additional 30 minutes or until rice is tender and liquid is absorbed, stirring after 15 minutes. Stir in pecans. Yield: 12 servings.

Sprinkle ground cinnamon over servings of Gingerbread with Raspberries and Cream; molasses gives this sweet cake lots of old-fashioned flavor.

Summer Squash Stir-Fry

¼ cup vegetable oil
2 cloves garlic, minced
2 medium onions, sliced and
  separated into rings
6 medium zucchini, thinly
  sliced
6 medium-size yellow squash,
  thinly sliced
16 cherry tomatoes, cut in half
1 teaspoon salt
1 teaspoon pepper
½ cup grated Parmesan cheese

Pour 2 tablespoons oil around top of preheated wok, coating sides; heat at medium high (325°) for 1 minute. Add 1 garlic clove and 1 onion; stir-fry 1 minute. Add 3 zucchini and 3 yellow squash; stir-fry 3 minutes or until crisp-tender. Add 8 cherry tomatoes, ½ teaspoon salt, and ½ teaspoon pepper; stir-fry 1 minute or until thoroughly heated. Transfer to a serving bowl, and keep warm. Repeat procedure with remaining ingredients except cheese. Sprinkle with cheese, and serve immediately. Yield: 12 servings.

Gingerbread with Raspberries and Cream

2¾ cups all-purpose flour
1 tablespoon ground ginger
1 teaspoon baking soda
¾ teaspoon salt
¾ teaspoon ground nutmeg
½ teaspoon ground cinnamon
¼ teaspoon ground cloves
1 cup light molasses
½ cup butter or margarine
½ cup firmly packed brown sugar
¾ cup buttermilk
2 eggs, beaten
2 tablespoons orange juice
2 tablespoons brandy
3 cups fresh raspberries
1 cup whipping cream
2 tablespoons sifted powdered
  sugar
Additional ground cinnamon

Combine first 7 ingredients, stirring well. Combine molasses, butter, and brown sugar in a saucepan. Cook over medium heat until butter melts and sugar dissolves, stirring constantly. Let cool slightly; add to flour mixture. Stir in buttermilk, eggs, juice, and brandy. Stir until smooth.

Pour batter into a greased and floured 13- x 9- x 2-inch baking pan. Bake at 350° for 25 to 30 minutes or until a wooden pick inserted in center comes out clean. Cool in pan 10 minutes. Let cool completely in pan on a wire rack. Cut into 12 squares. Top each serving with ¼ cup raspberries.

Beat whipping cream until soft peaks form. Add powdered sugar, beating until stiff peaks form. Spoon a dollop of whipped cream onto each serving. Sprinkle with cinnamon. Yield: 12 servings.

Cozy Sunday Supper

End a lazy Sunday afternoon by gathering friends for this satisfying meal. Spark interest by offering Smoked Oyster Spread with a tart white wine. Afterwards, start dinner with Country Garden Salad and Classic Breadsticks; then savor Chicken Pot Pies with Puff Pastry Crusts along with a rich, tart red wine. Complete the evening with a generous helping of Blueberry Crumble with Cold Custard Sauce.

Cozy Sunday Supper

Smoked Oyster Spread

Tiefenbrunner Pinot Grigio

Country Garden Salad

Classic Breadsticks

Chicken Pot Pies with
Puff Pastry Crusts

Fetzer Zinfandel-Special Reserve

Blueberry Crumble with
Cold Custard Sauce

Coffee

Serves six

Smoked Oyster Spread

1½ teaspoons unflavored gelatin
¼ cup cold water
½ (8-ounce) package cream
 cheese
½ cup mayonnaise
1 (3.66-ounce) can smoked
 oysters, drained and minced
2 tablespoons chopped
 pimiento-stuffed olives
1 teaspoon lemon juice
¼ teaspoon garlic powder
Dash of hot sauce
Sprigs of fresh parsley (optional)
Lemon twists (optional)

Soften gelatin in water in a small saucepan; cook over low heat, stirring until dissolved. Remove from heat, and set aside.

Combine cream cheese and mayonnaise in a saucepan; cook over low heat, stirring constantly, until cream cheese melts and mixture is smooth. Stir in oysters and next 4 ingredients. Stir in gelatin mixture; spoon oyster mixture into a greased 1½-cup mold. Cover and chill at least 8 hours. Unmold onto a serving plate. If desired, garnish with parsley and lemon twists; serve with crackers. Yield: 1½ cups.

Country Garden Salad

½ pound fresh green beans
1 small yellow squash, thinly
    sliced
1 small carrot, scraped and thinly
    sliced
1 head leaf lettuce, torn into
    bite-size pieces
1 small cucumber, thinly sliced
1 cup cherry tomatoes, halved
1 (8-ounce) package frozen baby
    corn, thawed
¼ cup red wine vinegar
2 tablespoons vegetable oil
2 tablespoons olive oil
1 teaspoon dried whole dillweed
1 teaspoon Dijon mustard
¼ teaspoon salt

Wash beans; trim ends, and re-move strings. Cut beans into 1-inch pieces. Arrange beans, squash, and carrot in a vegetable steamer over boiling water. Cover and steam 6 to 8 minutes or until vegetables are crisp-tender. Drain; rinse in cold water, and drain again.

Combine steamed vegetables, let-tuce, cucumber, cherry tomatoes, and corn in a large bowl, tossing gently. Combine vinegar and re-maining ingredients in a small bowl; stir with a wire whisk until blended. Drizzle vinegar mixture over salad, and toss gently. Yield: 6 servings.

Country Garden Salad contains lots of crisp vegetables—green beans, squash, carrots, cucumber, cherry tomatoes, lettuce, and ears of baby corn.

Classic Breadsticks

1 package dry yeast
2 teaspoons sugar
1¼ cups warm water (105° to
    115°)
3 to 3½ cups all-purpose flour,
    divided

1½ teaspoons salt
Cornmeal
1 egg white

Dissolve yeast and sugar in water in a large mixing bowl; let stand 5 minutes. Gradually add 1½ cups flour and salt, beating at low speed of an electric mixer until moistened. Increase to high speed; beat 3 minutes. Add enough remaining flour to make a stiff dough.

Turn dough out onto a well-floured surface, and knead until smooth and elastic (5 to 8 minutes). Place in a greased bowl, turning to grease top. Cover and let rise in a warm place (85°), free from drafts, 1 hour or until doubled in bulk. Punch dough down, and turn out onto a lightly floured surface. Knead several times until smooth. Let dough rest 10 minutes. Grease two baking sheets; sprinkle with cornmeal, and set aside.

Divide dough into fourths. Cut each fourth into 8 equal portions, using a pair of kitchen shears. Roll each portion into a 9-inch rope. Place ropes about 1 inch apart on prepared baking sheets. Brush with half of egg white. Let rise in a warm place, free from drafts, 30 minutes or until doubled in bulk. Brush with remaining egg white. Place a shallow pan containing 1 inch of water on bottom rack of oven; place baking sheets on top rack. Bake at 400° for 15 minutes or until breadsticks are golden brown. Yield: 32 breadsticks.

Chicken Pot Pies with Puff Pastry Crusts

1 cup chopped onion
1 cup chopped celery
1 cup chopped carrot
¼ cup plus 2 tablespoons butter
   or margarine, melted
1 cup frozen tiny English peas
¼ cup plus 2 tablespoons
   all-purpose flour
2 cups chicken broth
1 cup half-and-half
1 teaspoon salt
¼ teaspoon pepper
4 cups diced cooked chicken
2 (17¼-ounce) packages frozen
   puff pastry, thawed
1 egg yolk
1 tablespoon half-and-half

Sauté onion, celery, and carrot in butter in a large skillet 10 minutes. Stir in peas and flour; cook 1 minute, stirring constantly. Gradually add chicken broth and 1 cup half-and-half; cook over medium heat, stirring constantly, until mixture is thickened and bubbly. Stir in salt and pepper. Add diced chicken, stirring well. Ladle chicken mixture into six 10-ounce ovenproof soup bowls, filling to within ¾-inch of rim. Set bowls aside.

Roll pastry sheets to ⅛-inch thickness. Cut 6 circles of pastry, ½-inch larger than top rims of soup bowls. (Reserve any remaining pastry to make decorative designs for tops of pies, if desired.) Combine egg yolk and 1 tablespoon half-and-half, stirring well. Brush one side of each circle with egg mixture. Place pastry circles, brushed side down, over each bowl, folding edges under, and pressing firmly to sides of bowl to seal. Place any decorative designs on top. Brush top of each with remaining half of egg mixture. Place pies on a jellyroll pan or a large baking sheet. Bake at 400° for 15 to 20 minutes or until tops are puffed and browned. Serve immediately. Yield: 6 servings.

Blueberry Crumble with Cold Custard Sauce

4½ cups fresh or frozen
   blueberries, thawed
½ cup sugar
1 tablespoon lemon juice
½ cup quick-cooking oats,
   uncooked
½ cup all-purpose flour
½ cup firmly packed brown sugar
1 teaspoon ground cinnamon
¼ cup butter or margarine,
   softened
Cold Custard Sauce
Fresh strawberries (optional)
Sprigs of fresh mint (optional)

Combine blueberries, ½ cup sugar, and lemon juice; place in a lightly greased 8-inch square baking dish. Combine oats, flour, brown sugar, and cinnamon; cut in butter with a pastry blender until mixture resembles coarse meal. Sprinkle over berry mixture. Bake at 350° for 35 minutes. Serve warm or cold in individual bowls, and top with Cold Custard Sauce. If desired, garnish with fresh strawberries and sprigs of mint. Yield: 6 servings.

Cold Custard Sauce

2 cups milk
¼ cup plus 2 tablespoons
   sugar, divided
2 egg yolks
2 tablespoons cornstarch
½ teaspoon vanilla extract

Combine milk and ¼ cup sugar in a small saucepan; heat until sugar melts, stirring occasionally (do not boil). Remove from heat.

Combine egg yolks and remaining 2 tablespoons sugar in a medium bowl; gradually add cornstarch, stirring well. Gradually stir half of hot milk mixture into egg mixture; add to remaining hot milk mixture, stirring constantly. Cook over medium heat, stirring constantly, until mixture is smooth and thickened. Stir in vanilla. Pour into a small bowl; cover and chill. Yield: 2 cups.

These individual Chicken Pot Pies with Puff Pastry Crusts are filled with a creamy mixture of chicken and vegetables. The crusts turn a lovely golden brown upon baking.

Casual
Supper Club

When supper club meets at your house, select a Cajun buffet theme. Coconut Shrimp with Sweet Dipping Sauce and plenty of cold beer will get the evening started. Dinner features Orange, Onion, and Spinach Salad, Red Beans and Sausage with Rice, French Bread Loaves, and a spicy, peppery-flavored red wine. Top off the meal and the evening with a slice of Chocolate Marbled Terrine and a cup of Flaming Brandied Coffee.

145

Casual Supper Club

Coconut Shrimp with
Sweet Dipping Sauce

Pilsner Urquell Beer

———

Orange, Onion, and Spinach Salad

Red Beans and Sausage with Rice

French Bread Loaves

Côtes du Rhône Villages-Cairanne

———

Chocolate Marbled Terrine

Flaming Brandied Coffee

Serves six

Coconut Shrimp with Sweet Dipping Sauce

**2 pounds unpeeled medium-size
    fresh shrimp**
2 cups all-purpose flour, divided
1 (12-ounce) can beer
½ teaspoon baking powder
½ teaspoon paprika
½ teaspoon curry powder
¼ teaspoon salt
¼ teaspoon ground red pepper
**1 (14-ounce) package flaked
    coconut**
Vegetable oil
Sweet Dipping Sauce

Peel and devein shrimp, leaving tails intact.

Combine 1½ cups flour, beer, and next 5 ingredients. Dredge shrimp in remaining ½ cup flour, dip in beer batter, and roll in coconut. Fry shrimp in deep hot oil (350°) until coconut is golden brown. Serve shrimp with Sweet Dipping Sauce. Yield: 6 servings.

Sweet Dipping Sauce

**1 (10-ounce) jar orange
    marmalade**
**3 tablespoons prepared
    horseradish**
3 tablespoons Creole mustard

Combine all ingredients, stirring until smooth. Yield: 1¼ cups.

The spicy taste of Coconut Shrimp with Sweet Dipping Sauce is complemented by a golden, caramel-flavored beer.

Orange, Onion, and Spinach Salad

½ pound fresh spinach
2 small purple onions, thinly
 sliced
1 (11-ounce) can mandarin
 oranges, drained
¼ cup chopped celery

½ cup sugar
⅔ cup vegetable oil
¼ cup vinegar
1 tablespoon poppyseeds
1 teaspoon prepared mustard
½ teaspoon salt

Remove stems from spinach; wash leaves thoroughly, and pat dry. Combine spinach and next 3 ingredients in a large salad bowl, tossing gently. Combine sugar, oil, vinegar, poppyseeds, mustard, and salt in a jar. Cover tightly, and shake vigorously. Serve dressing with salad. Yield: 6 servings.

Red Beans and Sausage with Rice

1 pound dried red kidney beans
1 small ham hock
2 cups chopped onion
1½ cups chopped celery
1½ cups chopped green pepper
½ cup chopped green onions
1 (8-ounce) can tomato sauce
1 teaspoon garlic powder
1 teaspoon dried whole oregano
1 teaspoon dried whole thyme
½ teaspoon white pepper
½ teaspoon ground red pepper
½ teaspoon black pepper
2 bay leaves
2 to 3 dashes of hot sauce
1 pound smoked sausage, sliced
 diagonally into ¾-inch pieces
Hot cooked rice

Sort and wash beans; place in a large Dutch oven. Cover with water 2 inches above beans; let soak 8 hours. Drain. Cover beans with water, and add ham hock; bring to a boil. Cover, reduce heat, and simmer 45 minutes.

Add onion and remaining ingredients except sausage and rice; stir well. Cover and cook over low heat 1 hour, stirring occasionally. Add sausage to bean mixture. Cook, uncovered, over low heat 45 minutes, stirring occasionally. Remove and discard bay leaves. Serve bean mixture over rice. Yield: 6 servings.

French Bread Loaves

1 package dry yeast
1 teaspoon sugar
2 cups warm water (105° to
   115°), divided
2 teaspoons salt
6 cups unbleached all-purpose
   flour, divided
3 tablespoons cornmeal

Dissolve yeast and sugar in ¼ cup warm water in a large bowl; let stand 5 minutes. Add remaining 1¾ cups water, salt, and 4 cups flour to yeast mixture; beat at medium speed of an electric mixer until smooth. Stir in enough remaining flour to make a soft dough. Turn dough out onto a lightly floured surface, and knead until small bubbles form just under surface (about 15 minutes). Place dough in a well-greased bowl, turning to grease top. Cover and let rise in a warm place (85°), free from drafts, 1 hour or until dough is doubled in bulk.

Grease 3 French bread loafpans; sprinkle evenly with cornmeal, and set aside.

Punch dough down; cover and let rest 10 minutes. Divide dough into thirds. On a lightly floured surface, flatten each portion to an oval. Fold dough over lengthwise, and flatten with open hand. Fold it again, and roll with palms of hand into a 16- x 2-inch rope; place ropes of dough in prepared pans.

Cover pans tightly with plastic wrap, and let rise in a warm place, free from drafts, 25 minutes or until loaves are almost doubled in bulk. Gently cut ¼-inch-deep slits at intervals on loaves with a razor blade or sharp knife.

Place loaves in oven; spray loaves with water. Bake at 450° for 15 minutes, spraying every 3 minutes without removing bread from oven. Continue to bake, without spraying, 5 to 10 minutes or until loaves are golden and sound hollow when tapped. Yield: 3 loaves.

Chocolate Marbled Terrine

9 ounces white chocolate, coarsely chopped
¼ cup butter, cut into pieces
¼ cup whipping cream
2 teaspoons cognac
6 (1-ounce) squares semisweet chocolate, chopped
3 tablespoons butter, cut into pieces
¼ cup plus 2 tablespoons whipping cream
2 teaspoons Kahlúa or other coffee-flavored liqueur
2 egg whites
3 tablespoons sugar
Chocolate Syrup Sauce
Fresh raspberries (optional)
Sprigs of fresh mint (optional)

Lightly butter a 4½-cup terrine mold or loafpan, and line with plastic wrap; set aside.

Combine white chocolate and ¼ cup butter in top of a double boiler; bring water to a boil. Remove from heat, and stir gently until melted. Set white chocolate mixture aside to cool slightly. Gradually add ¼ cup whipping cream and cognac to white chocolate mixture, stirring well. Cover and let stand at room temperature 4 hours or until firm and cool (do not refrigerate).

Combine chopped semisweet chocolate and 3 tablespoons butter in top of double boiler; bring water to a boil. Remove from heat, and stir until chocolate and butter are melted. Set mixture aside to cool slightly. Gradually stir in ¼ cup plus 2 tablespoons whipping cream and Kahlúa. Cover and let stand at room temperature 2 hours or until mixture is firm (do not refrigerate).

Combine egg whites and 3 tablespoons sugar in top of a double boiler. Bring water to a boil. Whisk gently 1 to 2 minutes or until sugar dissolves. Remove from heat, and beat egg white mixture at medium speed of an electric mixer 7 minutes or until stiff peaks form and meringue mixture is cool. Set aside.

Beat white chocolate mixture at medium speed of electric mixer 3 minutes. Beat semisweet chocolate mixture at medium speed of electric mixer 3 minutes. Fold two-thirds of meringue mixture into white chocolate mixture. Fold remaining meringue mixture into chocolate mixture. Spoon white chocolate mixture into a large bowl; spoon chocolate mixture on top. Gently swirl mixture with 4 turns of a spatula to create marble effect. Carefully pour mixture into prepared mold. Cover with plastic wrap, and chill mixture at least 8 hours.

Wrap mold in a hot, damp cloth. Invert mold onto a cutting board; remove plastic wrap. Cut terrine into 1-inch slices with a warm, dry knife. Spoon cooled Chocolate Syrup Sauce onto each dessert plate, and gently place terrine slices over sauce. If desired, garnish with fresh raspberries and sprigs of fresh mint. Yield: 6 servings.

Chocolate Syrup Sauce

4 (1-ounce) squares semisweet chocolate
3 tablespoons butter
½ cup sifted powdered sugar
¼ cup plus 2 tablespoons light corn syrup
3 tablespoons water
½ teaspoon vanilla extract

Combine chocolate and butter in top of a double boiler; bring water to a boil. Reduce heat to low; cook until melted. Add remaining ingredients. Cook, stirring frequently, until smooth. Remove from heat; cover and cool. Yield: 1⅓ cups.

Flaming Brandied Coffee

¾ cup apricot brandy
6 cups hot coffee
2 tablespoons sugar
½ cup whipping cream, whipped
Ground nutmeg

Rinse beverage glass with hot water; dry. Pour 2 tablespoons brandy into glass. Rotate glass over flame of Irish coffee burner until brandy ignites. Fill glass with 1 cup coffee; stir in 1 teaspoon sugar. Top with whipped cream; sprinkle with nutmeg. Repeat procedure for each serving. Yield: 6 servings.

For a special dessert, serve Chocolate Marbled Terrine with Flaming Brandied Coffee. Just one bite of the terrine makes it worth the effort it takes to prepare.

Poolside
Supper

A hot, humid evening becomes fun when guests surround the pool for this buffet dinner. Cover tables with striped cloths; add terra-cotta accessories and rented folding chairs, and use hand towels for napkins. As everyone arrives, serve Crab-Stuffed Mushrooms and a light white wine. Guests can help themselves to Watermelon-Nut Salad, Honey-Glazed Flank Steak, Lemon Noodles with Asparagus and Pine Nuts, and Baby Carrots with Horseradish. Offer a full-flavored red wine, and follow up with Toasted Coconut Ice Cream and Crisp Oat Cookies.

Poolside Supper

Crab-Stuffed Mushrooms

Mâcon-Villages-Georges Duboeuf

———

Watermelon-Nut Salad

Honey-Glazed Flank Steak

Lemon Noodles with
Asparagus and Pine Nuts

Baby Carrots with Horseradish

Inglenook Merlot-Reserve

———

Toasted Coconut Ice Cream

Crisp Oat Cookies

Water

Serves eight

Crab-Stuffed Mushrooms

24 large fresh mushrooms
1 cup commercial Italian salad
   dressing
1 cup fresh lump crabmeat,
   drained and flaked
2 eggs, beaten
⅓ cup soft breadcrumbs
¼ cup mayonnaise
¼ cup minced green onions
2 tablespoons diced pimiento
1 teaspoon lemon juice
Sprigs of fresh dillweed or
   parsley

Clean mushrooms with damp paper towels. Remove stems, and reserve for other uses. Combine mushroom caps and Italian salad dressing; cover and chill 1 to 2 hours. Drain well.

Combine crabmeat and next 6 ingredients, stirring well. Spoon crabmeat mixture into mushroom caps. Place stuffed mushrooms in a lightly greased 13- x 9- x 2-inch baking dish; bake at 375° for 15 minutes. Garnish with fresh dillweed or parsley sprigs, and serve immediately. Yield: 2 dozen.

Guests will be eager to sample Baby Carrots with Horseradish, Lemon Noodles with Asparagus and Pine Nuts, Watermelon-Nut Salad, and Honey-Glazed Flank Steak.

Watermelon-Nut Salad

2 (3-ounce) packages cream
  cheese, softened
¼ cup mayonnaise
¼ cup marshmallow cream
2 tablespoons whipping cream
½ cup diced celery
⅓ cup finely chopped pecans,
  toasted
4 cups watermelon balls,
  chilled
3 tablespoons chopped pecans,
  toasted

Beat cream cheese at medium speed of an electric mixer until light and fluffy. Gradually add mayonnaise and marshmallow cream; beat mixture until smooth. Stir in whipping cream; add celery and ⅓ cup pecans, stirring well.

To serve, spoon watermelon balls onto individual salad plates. Spoon dressing mixture over melon, and sprinkle with 3 tablespoons pecans. Yield: 8 servings.

Honey-Glazed Flank Steak

2 (1¼-pound) flank steaks
½ cup vegetable oil
¼ cup plus 2 tablespoons
  honey
¼ cup soy sauce
1 teaspoon ground ginger
½ teaspoon garlic powder
Curly kale (optional)
Sprigs of fresh dillweed
  (optional)

Place steaks in a large shallow dish, and set aside.

Combine vegetable oil, honey, soy sauce, ginger, and garlic powder in a small bowl, stirring well.

Pour marinade mixture over steaks. Cover and marinate in the refrigerator 24 hours, turning steaks occasionally.

Remove steaks from marinade, and discard marinade. Grill steaks over hot coals 4 to 5 minutes on each side or to desired degree of doneness (steaks should be slightly rare). To serve, thinly slice steaks across the grain. If desired, garnish with curly kale and fresh dillweed sprigs. Yield: 8 servings.

Lemon Noodles with Asparagus and Pine Nuts

¾ cup half-and-half
¼ cup plus 2 tablespoons butter
  or margarine
1 pound fresh asparagus
  spears
1 (1-pound) package fettuccine

½ cup lemon juice
½ teaspoon grated lemon
  rind
⅓ cup grated Parmesan
  cheese
¼ cup pine nuts, toasted

Combine half-and-half and butter in a small saucepan. Cover and cook over low heat until butter melts; set aside, and keep warm.

Snap off tough ends of asparagus. Remove scales from stalks with a knife or vegetable peeler, if desired. Cut asparagus spears into 1½-inch pieces. Cover and cook in a small amount of boiling water 6 to 8 minutes or until crisp-tender. Drain well; set aside.

Cook fettuccine according to package directions; drain well. Place cooked fettuccine in a large bowl, and toss with lemon juice. Let fettuccine stand 1 minute. Add lemon rind, Parmesan cheese, toasted pine nuts, and asparagus to fettuccine. Add butter mixture, tossing gently. Serve immediately. Yield: 8 servings.

Baby Carrots with Horseradish

2½ pounds fresh baby carrots,
  with tops
¼ cup butter or margarine

⅓ cup honey
2 tablespoons prepared
  horseradish

Scrape carrots, leaving ¼ inch of green tops, if desired. Cook carrots, covered, in a small amount of boiling water over medium heat 18 to 20 minutes or until carrots are tender. Drain well.

Melt butter in a large saucepan over low heat; stir in honey and horseradish. Gently stir in carrots; cook until thoroughly heated. Serve carrots warm. Yield: 8 servings.

Toasted Coconut Ice Cream

5 cups milk
1¾ cups sugar
¼ cup plus 2 tablespoons
  all-purpose flour
½ teaspoon salt
5 eggs, beaten
3 cups half-and-half
1 (8.5-ounce) can cream of
  coconut
2 teaspoons vanilla extract
1 cup flaked coconut, toasted and
  lightly crushed
Additional toasted coconut

Heat milk in a 3-quart saucepan over low heat until thoroughly heated, but not boiling. Combine sugar, flour, and salt; gradually add sugar mixture to milk, stirring until blended. Cook over medium heat, stirring constantly, 15 to 20 minutes or until slightly thickened.

Gradually stir one-fourth of hot mixture into beaten eggs; add to remaining hot mixture, stirring constantly. Cook 1 minute; remove from heat. Chill at least 2 hours.

Combine half-and-half, cream of coconut, and vanilla in a large bowl; add chilled custard, stirring with a wire whisk to combine. Gently stir in 1 cup coconut. Pour mixture into freezer can of a 1-gallon hand-turned or electric freezer. Freeze according to manufacturer's instructions. Let ripen 2 hours before serving. Garnish with additional toasted coconut, if desired. Yield: 2½ quarts.

Crisp Oat Cookies

2 cups all-purpose flour
2 teaspoons baking soda
1 teaspoon baking powder
¼ teaspoon salt
1 cup shortening
1 cup firmly packed brown sugar
¾ cup sugar
2 eggs
1 teaspoon vanilla extract
2 cups quick-cooking oats,
  uncooked
1¾ cups corn flakes cereal

Combine flour, soda, baking powder, and salt; set aside.

Cream shortening; gradually add sugars, beating well at medium speed of an electric mixer. Add eggs and vanilla; beat well. Add flour mixture, mixing well. Stir in oats and corn flakes.

Shape dough into 1½-inch balls. Place on lightly greased cookie sheets, and flatten slightly. Bake at 325° for 12 to 14 minutes. Cool slightly on cookie sheets; remove to wire racks to cool completely. Yield: 3 dozen.

End the evening on a sweet note with Crisp Oat Cookies and Toasted Coconut Ice Cream.

Lunch for the Ladies

Set a feminine luncheon table with a pretty tablecloth, a cherub statue, flowers, and your finest china and crystal. The ladies will rave about the menu of Melon and Prosciutto with Honey Sauce, Cold Squash and Watercress Soup, Crab and Wild Rice Salad, Crescent Rolls, and blushing pink Rosé Spritzers. Dessert comes in the delightful form of Watermelon Sherbet and Vanilla Cookies.

Lunch for the Ladies

Melon and Prosciutto with
Honey Sauce

———

Cold Squash and Watercress Soup

Crab and Wild Rice Salad

Crescent Rolls

———

Watermelon Sherbet

Vanilla Cookies

———

Rosé Spritzers

Coffee

Serves four

Melon and Prosciutto with Honey Sauce

½ small ripe honeydew melon,
   seeded
8 thin slices prosciutto
2 tablespoons vegetable oil
1 tablespoon lime juice
1 tablespoon honey
½ teaspoon poppyseeds

Cut honeydew half into 8 thin lengthwise slices. Remove rind from each slice, using a sharp knife. Wrap one slice of prosciutto around each melon wedge. Set aside.

Combine oil, lime juice, honey, and poppyseeds in a small bowl; stir until smooth.

To serve, place two melon slices on each serving plate; drizzle melon slices with honey mixture. Yield: 4 servings.

Cold Squash and Watercress Soup

3 tablespoons butter or margarine
½ small onion, minced
⅛ teaspoon garlic powder
1 pound yellow squash, thinly sliced
1½ cups chicken broth
¼ cup chopped fresh watercress
½ cup half-and-half
¼ teaspoon salt
¼ teaspoon white pepper
4 thin slices yellow squash (optional)
Additional watercress (optional)

Melt butter in a large Dutch oven. Add onion and garlic powder; sauté until onion is tender. Stir in 1 pound squash, chicken broth, and ¼ cup watercress. Cover and simmer 10 to 15 minutes or until squash is tender.

Spoon half of squash mixture into container of an electric blender; top with cover, and process until smooth. Repeat procedure with remaining squash mixture. Transfer pureed mixture to a large bowl. Stir in half-and-half, salt, and pepper. Chill thoroughly. If desired, garnish with thin slices of yellow squash and additional watercress. Yield: 4 cups.

Crab and Wild Rice Salad

3 cups water
¾ pound unpeeled medium-size fresh shrimp
½ (4-ounce) package wild rice
12 ounces fresh lump crabmeat, drained
½ cup frozen tiny English peas, thawed
⅓ cup chopped green onions
1 (2-ounce) jar diced pimiento, drained
½ cup mayonnaise
1 tablespoon lemon juice
Leaf lettuce
Cherry tomatoes, cut into wedges

Bring water to a boil in a medium saucepan; add shrimp, and cook 3 minutes or until shrimp turn pink. Drain well; rinse with cold water. Peel and devein shrimp; set aside.

Cook rice according to package directions; let cool. Combine rice, shrimp, crabmeat, peas, onions, and pimiento; stir gently.

Combine mayonnaise and lemon juice. Gently stir into salad. Serve on lettuce leaves; garnish with cherry tomatoes. Yield: 4 cups.

The delicate flavor of Cold Squash and Watercress Soup is smooth and refreshing.

This ladylike luncheon menu features Crab and Wild Rice Salad, golden Crescent Rolls, and Rosé Spritzers.

Crescent Rolls

2 packages dry yeast
½ cup warm water (105° to 115°)
1 cup milk
¼ cup sugar
¼ cup butter or margarine
1 teaspoon salt
2 eggs, beaten
5½ to 6 cups all-purpose flour,
    divided
Melted butter or margarine

Dissolve yeast in warm water; let stand 5 minutes. Combine milk, sugar, ¼ cup butter, and salt in a saucepan; heat until butter melts. Cool to 105° to 115°. Add milk mixture, eggs, and 2 cups flour. Beat 2 minutes or until smooth. Gradually stir in enough remaining flour to make a soft dough.

Turn dough out onto a floured surface, and knead until smooth and elastic (8 to 10 minutes). Place in a well-greased bowl, turning to grease top. Cover and let rise in a warm place (85°), free from drafts, 45 minutes or until doubled in bulk.

Punch dough down; divide into thirds. Roll each portion to a 12-inch circle on a floured surface; brush with butter. Cut each circle into 12 wedges; roll up each wedge, beginning at wide end. Place on greased baking sheets, point side down. Curve into crescent shapes.

Cover and let rise in a warm place, free from drafts, 30 minutes or until rolls are doubled in bulk. Bake at 400° for 8 to 10 minutes or until lightly browned. Yield: 3 dozen.

Watermelon Sherbet

4½ cups seeded, diced
    watermelon
¾ cup sugar
1 tablespoon lemon juice
⅛ teaspoon salt
1 envelope unflavored gelatin
¼ cup cold water
1 cup whipping cream

Combine first 4 ingredients; chill 30 minutes. Spoon mixture into container of an electric blender. Top with cover; process until very smooth.

Sprinkle gelatin over cold water in a small saucepan; let stand 1 minute. Cook over low heat, stirring constantly, until gelatin dissolves. Add to watermelon mixture, stirring well. Add whipping cream, beating with a wire whisk until thoroughly combined. Pour mixture into freezer can of a 1-gallon hand-turned or electric freezer. Freeze according to manufacturer's instructions. Let ripen 1 hour before serving. Yield: 1½ quarts.

Vanilla Cookies

½ cup butter or margarine,
    softened
¾ cup sugar
¼ cup firmly packed brown sugar
1 egg
2 teaspoons vanilla extract
1¾ cups all-purpose flour
½ teaspoon baking soda
½ teaspoon salt
½ cup chopped walnuts

Cream butter; gradually add sugars, beating well. Add egg and vanilla; beat well. Combine flour, soda, and salt; add to creamed mixture, beating well. Stir in walnuts. Shape dough into four 9-inch rolls; wrap in wax paper, and chill 2 hours or until firm. Unwrap rolls, and cut into ½-inch slices. Place on ungreased cookie sheets; bake at 400° for 6 to 8 minutes or until lightly browned. Cool cookies slightly on cookie sheets; remove to wire racks to cool completely. Yield: about 6 dozen.

Note: Dough may be frozen up to 3 months.

Rosé Spritzers

1 (750-milliliter) bottle
    rosé wine
2 cups club soda
Lemon slices

Combine wine and club soda, stirring well. Pour into ice-filled glasses, and garnish with lemon slices. Yield: 5 cups.

Casual
Weekend
Lunch

Make the most of an overcast, warm day by moving everything outdoors where you can enjoy the view of the meadow and garden. Egg Dip with fresh vegetables will awaken the taste buds. The casual lunch of Cabbage Salad with French-Honey Dressing, Louisiana Gumbo, Buttermilk Corn Sticks, and a dry red wine is one you will want to linger over. Serve bowls of Fresh Peach Cobbler for dessert; it tastes so good, you will think your grandmother made it.

Casual Weekend Lunch

Egg Dip

———

Cabbage Salad with
French-Honey Dressing

Louisiana Gumbo

Buttermilk Corn Sticks

Beaujolais-Villages-Bouchard

———

Fresh Peach Cobbler

Coffee

———

Water

Serves eight

Egg Dip

1 (8-ounce) package cream
  cheese, softened
½ cup plus 2 tablespoons half-
  and-half
3 hard-cooked eggs, sieved
2 tablespoons mayonnaise
1 (0.7-ounce) envelope Italian
  salad dressing mix

Combine cream cheese and half-
and-half in a small mixing bowl; beat
at medium speed of an electric mixer
until creamy. Add eggs and remaining ingredients, mixing until light and
fluffy. Serve dip with fresh vegetables. Yield: 2⅓ cups.

Cabbage Salad with French-Honey Dressing

8 cups finely shredded cabbage
1 cup finely shredded carrots
1 cup vegetable oil
½ cup catsup
½ cup honey
⅓ cup cider vinegar
¾ teaspoon garlic salt
¾ teaspoon paprika

Combine cabbage and carrot in a
large bowl, tossing well. Cover and
chill thoroughly.

Combine oil and remaining ingredients in container of an electric
blender; top with cover, and process
on low speed 1 minute or until
smooth. Chill thoroughly. Drizzle
dressing over salad before serving.
Yield: 8 servings.

Louisiana Gumbo

½ cup vegetable oil
½ cup all-purpose flour
2 cups chopped onion
1½ cups chopped green pepper
1 cup chopped celery
1 clove garlic, minced
1 pound smoked sausage, cut into
  ¼-inch slices
¾ pound okra, sliced
4 cups chicken broth
4 cups water
2 cups peeled, chopped tomato
¼ cup Worcestershire sauce
¼ cup catsup
2 bay leaves
1 teaspoon garlic salt
1 teaspoon hot sauce
½ teaspoon ground red pepper
¼ teaspoon dried whole thyme
¼ teaspoon dried whole oregano
1 pound unpeeled medium-size
  fresh shrimp
1 pound fresh crabmeat, drained
  and flaked
2 cups chopped cooked chicken
1 (12-ounce) container fresh
  Standard oysters, undrained
Hot cooked rice
Gumbo filé (optional)

Combine oil and flour in a large Dutch oven; cook over medium heat, stirring constantly, until roux is caramel colored (15 to 20 minutes). Stir in onion, green pepper, celery, and minced garlic; cook 45 minutes, stirring occasionally.

Cook sausage in a large skillet until lightly browned; drain, reserving 1 tablespoon drippings in skillet.

Add sausage to onion mixture. Cook okra in pan drippings until browned. Add to onion mixture, stirring well. Cook over low heat until thoroughly heated. Add broth and water to onion mixture, stirring well. Add tomato and next 8 ingredients; reduce heat, and simmer 2 hours, stirring occasionally.

Peel and devein shrimp; add shrimp, crabmeat, chopped chicken, and oysters to vegetable mixture. Simmer 10 to 15 minutes or until edges of oysters begin to curl and shrimp is done. Remove and discard bay leaves. Serve gumbo over rice, and sprinkle with gumbo filé, if desired. Yield: 18 cups.

The spicy flavor of Louisiana Gumbo defies description. Just savor a bowl with some Buttermilk Corn Sticks and taste how good it is.

Buttermilk Corn Sticks

1½ cups yellow cornmeal
¼ cup all-purpose flour
2 teaspoons sugar
1 teaspoon baking powder
½ teaspoon baking soda

½ teaspoon salt
1 cup buttermilk
1 egg, beaten
2 tablespoons vegetable oil

Combine first 6 ingredients; stir in buttermilk and egg just until dry ingredients are moistened. Stir in oil. Place a well-greased cast-iron corn stick pan in a 400° oven for 3 minutes or until hot. Remove pan from oven; spoon batter into pan, filling two-thirds full. Bake at 400° for 12 to 15 minutes or until corn sticks are lightly browned. Yield: 14 corn sticks.

Fresh Peach Cobbler

8 cups sliced fresh peaches
1¼ cups sugar
⅓ cup firmly packed brown sugar
¼ cup all-purpose flour
1 teaspoon grated lemon rind
1 teaspoon vanilla extract
½ teaspoon ground cinnamon
¼ teaspoon ground ginger

⅓ cup butter or margarine, melted
2 cups all-purpose flour
1 teaspoon salt
⅔ cup plus 2 tablespoons shortening
3 to 4 tablespoons cold water
Vanilla ice cream (optional)

Combine first 8 ingredients in a large Dutch oven; set aside until mixture forms a syrup. Bring peach mixture to a boil; reduce heat to low, and cook, uncovered, 5 to 10 minutes or until peaches are tender. Remove from heat, and stir in butter.

Combine 2 cups flour and salt; cut in shortening with a pastry blender until mixture resembles coarse meal. Sprinkle cold water (1 tablespoon at a time) evenly over surface; stir with a fork until dry ingredients are moistened. Shape into a ball; chill.

Roll out half of dough to ⅛-inch thickness on a lightly floured surface; cut into a 11- x 7-inch rectangle. Spoon half of peach mixture into a greased 11- x 7- x 2-inch baking dish; top with pastry. Bake at 475° for 15 minutes. Top with remaining peach mixture. Roll out remaining dough to ⅛-inch thickness on a lightly floured surface, and cut into 1-inch strips; arrange in a lattice design over peaches. Bake at 475° for 18 to 20 minutes or until golden. Spoon cobbler into serving bowls; top each with a scoop of ice cream, if desired. Yield: 8 servings.

Fragrant peaches are one of the treasures of a Southern summer, and there is no better way to enjoy them than in Fresh Peach Cobbler.

Lunch in the Herb Garden

This fragrant herb garden is a setting that appeals to gardeners and culinary artists alike. The simple menu starts with Creamy Cucumber Soup served with a crisp white wine. Next is a salad plate of Fruited Chicken Salad, Granny's Potato Salad, and Flavorful Pasta Salad. Serve Zucchini Pickles and Herbed Cheese Twists on the side, along with a glass of a fruity, dry red wine. For dessert, offer Ginger-Cocoa Crisps—a delicious ending for a relaxed midday meal.

169

Lunch in the Herb Garden

Creamy Cucumber Soup

Frascati-Fontana Candida

Fruited Chicken Salad

Granny's Potato Salad

Flavorful Pasta Salad

Zucchini Pickles

Herbed Cheese Twists

Santa Sofia Valpolicella

Ginger-Cocoa Crisps

Coffee

Serves four

Creamy Cucumber Soup

1 cup half-and-half
1 (8-ounce) carton sour cream
1 (8-ounce) carton plain yogurt
2 cucumbers, peeled, seeded, and coarsely chopped
1 green onion, coarsely chopped
1 tablespoon minced fresh dillweed or ½ teaspoon dried whole dillweed
1 tablespoon lemon juice
1 tablespoon milk
½ teaspoon salt
¼ teaspoon white pepper
Dash of hot sauce
Sprigs of fresh dillweed (optional)

Combine first 11 ingredients in container of an electric blender or food processor; top with cover, and process just until smooth. Chill thoroughly. Stir well before serving; garnish with sprigs of dillweed, if desired. Yield: 4 servings.

If you like the cool flavor of cucumbers, then Creamy Cucumber Soup will be a favorite. This soup is best made ahead and chilled before serving.

Fruited Chicken Salad

1½ cups diced cooked chicken
2 tablespoons thinly sliced celery
2 tablespoons chopped green
   pepper
1 green onion, chopped
2 teaspoons lemon juice
½ cup halved seedless green
   grapes
½ cup mandarin oranges
3 tablespoons mayonnaise
2 tablespoons coarsely chopped
   pecans, toasted
⅛ teaspoon salt
Dash of pepper
Leaf lettuce

Combine first 5 ingredients; stir well. Cover and chill. Add grapes, oranges, mayonnaise, pecans, salt, and pepper to chicken mixture; toss well. Serve salad on leaf lettuce. Yield: 4 servings.

Granny's Potato Salad

4 medium-size red potatoes,
   unpeeled
1 hard-cooked egg, finely chopped
¼ cup mayonnaise
3 tablespoons sour cream
1 tablespoon chopped green
   onions
1 tablespoon commercial Italian
   salad dressing
½ teaspoon honey mustard
¼ teaspoon salt
⅛ teaspoon pepper
2 slices bacon
Leaf lettuce

Cook potatoes in boiling water to cover 20 to 25 minutes or until tender. Drain and cool slightly. Peel and cut potatoes into ¾-inch cubes. Combine potatoes and next 8 ingredients in a medium bowl, tossing gently. Set aside.

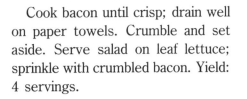

Cook bacon until crisp; drain well on paper towels. Crumble and set aside. Serve salad on leaf lettuce; sprinkle with crumbled bacon. Yield: 4 servings.

Flavorful Pasta Salad

1 cup uncooked corkscrew
   macaroni
2 green onions, choppcd
1 small carrot, thinly sliced
1 (2-ounce) jar diced pimiento,
   drained
¼ cup chopped green pepper
½ cup frozen English peas,
   thawed
8 cherry tomatoes, halved
⅓ cup commercial Italian salad
   dressing
⅛ teaspoon celery salt
⅛ tcaspoon white pepper
Leaf lettuce

Cook macaroni according to package directions, omitting salt; drain. Rinse with cold water; drain again.

Combine macaroni and remaining ingredients except lettuce, tossing well; cover and chill at least 1 hour. Serve salad on leaf lettuce, using a slotted spoon. Yield: 4 servings.

Zucchini Pickles

2 pounds medium zucchini, thinly
    sliced
2 small onions, thinly sliced
¼ cup pickling salt
2 teaspoons mustard seeds
1 teaspoon celery seeds
2 cups sugar
3 cups cider vinegar (5% acidity)

Layer zucchini, onion, and salt in a large glass container; add water to cover. Let stand 2 hours. Rinse and drain zucchini and onion 3 times in cold water. Drain vegetables well, and set aside.

Tie mustard seeds and celery seeds in a cheesecloth bag. Combine spice bag, sugar, and vinegar in a stainless steel Dutch oven; bring to a boil. Add zucchini and onion. Remove from heat; cover and let stand 2 hours. Bring to a boil; reduce heat, and simmer 5 minutes, stirring gently. Remove spice bag.

Pack hot vegetables into hot sterilized jars. Pour remaining vinegar mixture over vegetables, leaving ½-inch headspace. Remove air bubbles; wipe jar rims. Cover at once with metal lids, and screw on bands. Process pickles in boiling-water bath 10 minutes. Yield: 3 pints.

Herbed Cheese Twists

3 tablespoons butter or
    margarine, softened
¼ teaspoon garlic powder
¼ teaspoon dried whole oregano
⅛ teaspoon dried whole basil
1 (16-ounce) loaf frozen bread
    dough, thawed
½ cup (2 ounces) shredded
    mozzarella cheese
1 egg white
1 teaspoon water
1 tablespoon poppyseeds

Cream butter, garlic powder, oregano, and basil in a small bowl until smooth. Set aside.

Roll bread dough to a 12-inch square on a heavily floured surface. Spread butter mixture evenly over dough; sprinkle with cheese. Fold dough into thirds. Cut dough crosswise into 24 ½-inch-wide strips. Twist each strip twice, and pinch ends to seal. Place 2 inches apart on a lightly greased baking sheet. Cover and let rise in a warm place (85°), free from drafts, 30 minutes or until doubled in bulk.

Combine egg white and water in a small bowl, stirring well. Brush egg white mixture over each twist. Sprinkle lightly with poppyseeds. Bake at 375° for 10 to 12 minutes or until golden. Yield: 2 dozen.

Herbed Cheese Twists, frosted with poppyseeds, are delightful added to a luncheon salad plate.

Ginger-Cocoa Crisps

¾ cup shortening
1 cup sugar
1 egg
¼ cup molasses
2 cups all-purpose flour
¼ cup unsweetened cocoa
1½ teaspoons baking soda
2½ teaspoons ground ginger
½ teaspoon salt
¼ cup sugar

Cream shortening; gradually add 1 cup sugar, beating at medium speed of an electric mixer until light and fluffy. Add egg, and beat well. Stir in molasses. Sift flour and cocoa together; stir in soda, ginger, and salt. Add to creamed mixture, stirring well.

Shape dough into 1-inch balls; roll in ¼ cup sugar. Place 2 inches apart on lightly greased cookie sheets. Bake at 350° for 10 to 12 minutes. Cool cookies completely on wire racks. Yield: about 4 dozen.

Ginger-Cocoa Crisps resemble old-fashioned gingersnap cookies. The only difference is that these crisp cookies are flavored with cocoa.

Outdoor Wedding Lunch

Rent a tent and set up outdoors for this lovely, romantic occasion. Decorate bird cages with flowers for beautiful centerpieces. Begin the meal with dainty appetizers like Sweet Glazed Walnuts, Pickled Baby Vegetable Crudités, and a fruity red wine. A delightful Goat Cheese and Pear Salad with Dijon Dressing is followed by an appealing plate of Gingered Beef Tenderloin, Saffron and Red Pepper Rice, and Baked Tomato Cups. This menu calls for a full-bodied, fruity red wine. And for dessert, offer the tart taste of Pink Grapefruit Ice.

175

Outdoor Wedding Lunch

Sweet Glazed Walnuts

Pickled Baby Vegetable Crudités

Fleurie-Georges Duboeuf

Goat Cheese and Pear Salad
with Dijon Dressing

Gingered Beef Tenderloin

Saffron and Red Pepper Rice

Baked Tomato Cups

*William Hill
Cabernet Sauvignon-Reserve*

Pink Grapefruit Ice

Coffee

Water

Serves twelve

Sweet Glazed Walnuts

2 cups sugar
½ cup water
½ cup orange juice
1 teaspoon ground cinnamon
½ teaspoon ground allspice
4 cups walnut halves
2 teaspoons vanilla extract

Combine first 5 ingredients in a Dutch oven. Cook over medium heat 5 minutes or until sugar dissolves, stirring constantly. Add walnuts, and continue to cook until mixture reaches soft ball stage (234°), stirring occasionally. Remove mixture from heat; stir in vanilla. Place walnuts on wax paper, and separate with a fork. Cool completely. Yield: 4 cups.

Pickled Baby Vegetable Crudités

2 pounds baby carrots
½ pound miniature yellow squash
½ pound miniature zucchini
2 quarts water
¾ cup pickling salt
3 cups cider vinegar (5% acidity)
1 cup water
½ cup sugar
2 tablespoons mixed pickling spices
1 teaspoon whole peppercorns
4 cloves garlic
2 dried whole red peppers
Sprigs of fresh dillweed (optional)

Lightly scrape carrots, leaving ¼-inch of tops, if desired. Wash squash and zucchini.

Combine 2 quarts water and salt in a large bowl; stir until salt dissolves. Add vegetables; cover and let stand at room temperature 24 hours. Rinse vegetables several times in cold water; drain well.

Combine vinegar, 1 cup water, sugar, pickling spices, and peppercorns in a large saucepan. Bring mixture to a boil; boil 10 minutes.

Pack vegetables evenly into hot sterilized jars, leaving ½-inch headspace. Add 2 cloves garlic and a red pepper to each jar. Pour boiling vinegar mixture over vegetables, leaving ½-inch headspace. Cover at once with metal lids, and screw on bands. Process in boiling-water bath 10 minutes. Let cool. Serve vegetables on a tray lined with fresh dillweed, if desired. Yield: 2 quarts.

Goat Cheese and Pear Salad with Dijon Dressing

1 cup olive oil
1 tablespoon dried whole basil
1 tablespoon chopped fresh chives
4 (3.5-ounce) logs Sonoma or Montrachet goat cheese
¾ cup soft breadcrumbs, toasted
4 cups torn Bibb lettuce
4 cups torn radicchio
4 cups torn romaine lettuce
2 (16-ounce) cans pear halves, drained and diced
1 medium-size green pepper, diced
¾ cup chopped walnuts
Dijon Dressing

Combine first 3 ingredients in a large, shallow dish; stir well. Slice cheese into 24 rounds; place in olive oil mixture. Cover and chill at least 6 hours. Drain cheese, and coat each slice with breadcrumbs. Place cheese on a baking sheet. Bake at 400° for 10 minutes or until lightly browned. Cool.

Combine lettuce; place 1 cup lettuce leaves on each salad plate. Arrange two cheese slices on each plate. Sprinkle with diced pear, green pepper, and walnuts. Drizzle Dijon Dressing over each serving. Yield: 12 servings.

Dijon Dressing

¼ cup plus 2 tablespoons white wine vinegar
2 tablespoons finely chopped green onions
2 tablespoons finely chopped fresh parsley
1 tablespoon plus 1 teaspoon Dijon mustard
½ teaspoon salt
½ teaspoon pepper
1 cup walnut oil

Combine first 6 ingredients in a small bowl; gradually add oil in a slow, steady stream, beating with a wire whisk. Cover and chill. Whisk dressing again just before serving. Yield: 1½ cups.

For an interesting appetizer, offer Pickled Baby Vegetable Crudités served on a bed of fresh dillweed. The tart flavor of the vegetables pairs perfectly with a light, fruity red wine.

Gingered Beef Tenderloin

1½ cups water
1 cup catsup
1 tablespoon ground ginger
1 tablespoon grated fresh
   gingerroot
½ teaspoon Worcestershire sauce
1 (6-pound) beef tenderloin,
   trimmed
Sprigs of fresh parsley (optional)

Combine first 5 ingredients; stir well. Pierce meat in several places, using a meat fork; place in a zip-top heavy-duty plastic bag. Pour marinade into bag, and seal tightly. Place bag in a shallow pan, and chill 8 hours, turning occasionally.

Drain marinade into a small saucepan. Cook over low heat just until thoroughly heated; set marinade aside. Place tenderloin on a rack in a baking pan; insert meat thermometer, making sure it does not touch fat. Bake tenderloin at 425° for 30 to 45 minutes or until meat thermometer registers 140°, basting meat occasionally with marinade. Remove meat to a serving platter. Garnish with sprigs of parsley, if desired. Yield: 12 servings.

Saffron and Red Pepper Rice

2½ cups chicken broth
2 tablespoons butter or margarine
1 teaspoon salt
¼ teaspoon ground turmeric
⅛ teaspoon ground saffron

2 cups uncooked long-grain rice
1 (10-ounce) package frozen
   English peas
1 cup diced sweet red pepper
¼ cup chopped green onions

Combine first 5 ingredients in a large heavy saucepan; bring to a boil. Gradually add rice, stirring constantly. Cover, reduce heat, and simmer 10 minutes. Stir in English peas, sweet red pepper, and green onions; cover and simmer an additional 10 minutes or until rice is tender. Yield: 12 servings.

Baked Tomato Cups

6 medium tomatoes, halved
   crosswise
¼ cup Dijon mustard
¼ teaspoon salt
¼ cup plus 2 tablespoons
   Italian-seasoned breadcrumbs

¼ cup plus 2 tablespoons grated
   Parmesan cheese
¼ cup butter or margarine,
   melted
½ teaspoon dried parsley flakes
⅛ teaspoon ground red pepper

Lightly brush cut surface of tomato halves with mustard. Place tomato halves, cut side up, in a 13- x 9- x 2-inch baking dish; sprinkle with salt.

Combine breadcrumbs and remaining ingredients in a small bowl; stir well. Top each tomato half with 1 tablespoon crumb mixture, spreading evenly. Bake at 350° for 10 minutes or until tomatoes are thoroughly heated and cheese melts. Place tomatoes under broiler; broil 2 to 3 minutes or until tops are golden. Yield: 12 servings.

A colorful plate can be arranged with sliced Gingered Beef Tenderloin, Saffron and Red Pepper Rice, and a Baked Tomato Cup.

Pink Grapefruit Ice

1¼ cups sugar
2 cups water
⅓ cup minced fresh mint leaves
5 cups pink grapefruit juice
   cocktail
2 tablespoons grenadine syrup

Combine sugar, water, and mint in a small saucepan; bring to a boil. Boil 5 minutes, stirring occasionally, until sugar dissolves. Remove from heat; strain, discarding mint. Let mixture cool.

Combine sugar mixture, grapefruit juice cocktail, and grenadine syrup in a large bowl, stirring until blended. Pour mixture into a 13- x 9- x 2-inch baking pan; cover and freeze until firm.

Break frozen mixture into large pieces. Position knife blade in food processor bowl; add frozen mixture to processor bowl in batches. Top with cover, and process until fluffy, but not thawed. Serve immediately. Yield: about 9 cups.

Beside a
Country Lake

The warm sun and gentle breeze turn this dockside feast into one to remember. Pull up a lounge chair and enjoy Fried Dill Pickles, Chili Fried Chicken, Vegetable-Rice Toss, Stuffed Yellow Squash, Spiced Peaches, and Cornbread Wheel. For dessert, relish Individual Strawberry Shortcakes. For total contentment, wash it all down with large glasses of iced Mint Tea.

Beside a Country Lake

Fried Dill Pickles

Chili Fried Chicken

Vegetable-Rice Toss

Stuffed Yellow Squash

Spiced Peaches

Cornbread Wheel

Individual Strawberry Shortcakes

Mint Tea

Serves four

Fried Dill Pickles

1 egg, beaten
½ cup milk
½ cup beer
1 tablespoon all-purpose flour
3 drops of hot sauce
3 cups all-purpose flour
2 teaspoons ground red pepper
1 teaspoon pepper
½ teaspoon salt
¼ teaspoon garlic powder
2 pints sliced dill pickles, drained
Vegetable oil

Combine egg, milk, beer, 1 tablespoon flour, and hot sauce in a medium bowl; stir well. Combine 3 cups flour and next 4 ingredients,

stirring well. Dip pickle slices in egg mixture; dredge in flour mixture. Fry pickles in deep hot oil (375°) for 5 minutes or until browned. Drain on paper towels, and serve immediately. Yield: 10 dozen.

Chili Fried Chicken

1½ cups all-purpose flour
1 tablespoon ground red pepper
1 teaspoon chili powder
1 teaspoon pepper
½ teaspoon poultry seasoning
½ cup milk
1 egg, beaten
1 (3- to 3½-pound) broiler-fryer, cut up
Vegetable oil

Combine first 5 ingredients in a zip-top heavy-duty plastic bag; shake to mix, and set aside.

Combine milk and egg in a shallow dish; stir well.

Place 2 or 3 pieces of chicken in bag; shake well. Dip chicken in egg mixture; return to bag, and shake again. Repeat procedure with remaining chicken.

Heat 1 inch of oil in an electric skillet to 325°; add chicken, and fry 20 to 25 minutes or until browned, turning once. Drain chicken on paper towels. Yield: 4 servings.

Vegetable-Rice Toss, a colorful combination, is ideal to take on an outdoor adventure.

Vegetable-Rice Toss

½ cup peeled, diced cucumber
½ cup diced carrot
⅓ cup frozen English peas
¼ cup chopped green onions
2 tablespoons diced pimiento
1 cup cooked long-grain rice, chilled
1 tablespoon plus 1½ teaspoons cider vinegar
¼ teaspoon salt
Dash of hot sauce
1 tablespoon plus 1½ teaspoons vegetable oil
Leaf lettuce

Press cucumber between paper towels to remove excess moisture; set cucumber aside.

Combine carrot and peas in a small saucepan; cover with water, and cook 3 to 5 minutes or just until crisp-tender. Drain and rinse with cold water.

Combine cucumber, carrot, peas, onions, pimiento, and rice in a medium bowl. Combine vinegar, salt, hot sauce, and oil in a small bowl; beat with a wire whisk until blended. Pour vinegar mixture over rice mixture, and toss gently. Serve on lettuce leaves. Yield: 4 servings.

Stuffed Yellow Squash

4 medium-size yellow squash
3 slices bacon
4 green onions, chopped
1 teaspoon grated green pepper
¾ cup fine, dry breadcrumbs
½ teaspoon pepper
¼ teaspoon salt
3 tablespoons butter or margarine, melted
2 tablespoons plus 2 teaspoons grated Parmesan cheese

Wash squash thoroughly. Place squash in a large saucepan. Cover with water; bring water to a boil. Cover, reduce heat, and simmer 10 minutes or until squash are tender, but still firm. Drain and cool slightly; trim off stems. Cut squash in half lengthwise; remove and reserve pulp, leaving a firm shell. Set squash shells aside.

Fry bacon until crisp; remove from pan, and drain on paper towels. Crumble bacon. Drain off bacon drippings, reserving 1½ teaspoons in pan. Add onions and green pepper; sauté in drippings until tender.

Combine squash pulp, bacon, onions, green pepper, breadcrumbs, pepper, salt, and butter; stir well. Spoon mixture into squash shells. Place in a 13- x 9- x 2-inch baking dish. Sprinkle squash with cheese. Broil 4 inches from heat 3 minutes or until lightly browned. Serve immediately. Yield: 4 servings.

Spiced Peaches

4 (4-inch) sticks cinnamon
2 tablespoons whole cloves
5 cups sugar, divided
3 cups vinegar
2 cups water
33 small, firm, ripe peaches, peeled

Tie cinnamon sticks and cloves together in a cheesecloth bag. Combine spice bag, 2 cups sugar, vinegar, and water in a large Dutch oven; bring to a boil. Add peaches; simmer 2 minutes or until thoroughly heated. Remove from heat; let stand 3 to 4 hours. Carefully remove peaches from syrup mixture; set peaches aside.

Add 2 cups sugar to syrup mixture; bring to a boil. Remove mixture from heat; add peaches. Cover and let stand 24 hours.

Heat peaches thoroughly in syrup mixture. Pack hot peaches into hot sterilized jars, leaving ½-inch headspace. Add remaining 1 cup sugar to syrup mixture; bring to a boil. Pour boiling syrup over peaches, leaving ½-inch headspace; wipe jar rims. Cover jars at once with metal lids, and screw on bands. Process peaches in boiling-water bath 20 minutes. Yield: 3 quarts.

Cornbread Wheel

¾ cup self-rising cornmeal
3 tablespoons all-purpose
   flour
2 teaspoons sugar
½ teaspoon baking soda
½ teaspoon salt
1 (8-ounce) carton sour cream
1 (7-ounce) can whole kernel
   corn with sweet peppers,
   drained
1 cup (4 ounces) shredded
   Cheddar cheese
2 eggs, beaten
3 jalapeño peppers, seeded
   and chopped
1 tablespoon vegetable oil

Combine cornmeal, flour, sugar, soda, and salt in a large bowl; stir well. Stir in sour cream and remaining ingredients.

Pour batter into a greased 9-inch cast-iron skillet. Bake at 350° for 50 to 55 minutes or until cornbread is golden. Cut into 8 wedges. Yield: 4 servings.

Individual Strawberry Shortcakes

2 cups fresh strawberries, hulled
   and sliced
2 tablespoons sugar
1 cup plus 3 tablespoons
   unbleached flour
1 tablespoon sugar
2 teaspoons baking powder
¼ teaspoon salt
2 tablespoons butter
¼ cup plus 2 tablespoons
   half-and-half
¾ cup whipping cream
2 teaspoons powdered sugar
4 strawberry fans (optional)

Combine 2 cups strawberries and 2 tablespoons sugar; stir gently. Cover and chill at least 45 minutes.

Combine flour and next 3 ingredients in a large bowl. Cut in butter with a pastry blender until mixture resembles coarse meal. Sprinkle half-and-half (1 tablespoon at a time) evenly over surface; stir with a fork until all ingredients are moistened. Shape dough into a ball. Roll dough to ⅝-inch thickness on a floured surface. Cut into four 3-inch circles. Place circles on a lightly greased baking sheet; bake at 450° for 10 minutes or until shortcakes are golden. Let cool completely on a wire rack.

Beat whipping cream at high speed of an electric mixer until foamy; gradually add powdered sugar, beating until soft peaks form. Split shortcakes horizontally. Place bottom half of each shortcake, cut side up, on each of 4 individual dessert plates; spoon half of whipped cream on bottom layers. Top with sweetened strawberries. Cover strawberries with top half of each shortcake, cut side down. Spoon on remaining whipped cream; garnish each shortcake with a strawberry fan, if desired. Yield: 4 servings.

Layers of whipped cream, flaky shortcake, and sweet strawberries make Individual Strawberry Shortcakes an all-time favorite Southern dessert.

Mint Tea

2 quart-size tea bags
1 cup sugar
¾ cup packed fresh mint
   leaves
Juice of 2 lemons
1 quart boiling water
1 quart cold water
Sprigs of fresh mint

Combine first 4 ingredients; pour boiling water over tea mixture. Cover and steep 5 to 10 minutes. Remove and discard tea bags and mint leaves. Transfer tea to a pitcher; add 1 quart cold water. Serve over ice. Garnish with sprigs of mint. Yield: 2 quarts.

Reflecting Pool Retreat

This calm, serene setting is a wonderful place to enjoy a gourmet-quality dinner. Begin by presenting guests with delicious Chutney-Cheese Pâté and Arugula, Endive, and Carrot Salad. Then offer attractively arranged plates of Blackened Breast of Duck, Green Beans in Raspberry Vinaigrette, and Twice-Baked Potato Spirals. Follow up with a full-bodied, fruity red wine. Everyone will agree that Pear Tart with Brandy Whip makes a lovely ending to a most enjoyable meal.

Reflecting Pool Retreat

Chutney-Cheese Pâté

Arugula, Endive, and Carrot Salad

Blackened Breast of Duck

Green Beans in Raspberry Vinaigrette

Twice-Baked Potato Spirals

Château Montelena Cabernet Sauvignon

Pear Tart with Brandy Whip

Coffee

Water

Serves four

Chutney-Cheese Pâté

1 cup (4 ounces) shredded
   Cheddar cheese
1 (3-ounce) package cream
   cheese, softened
¼ cup chopped green onions
2 tablespoons mayonnaise
½ teaspoon curry powder
¼ teaspoon garlic powder
⅛ teaspoon salt
½ cup chutney, chopped
2 tablespoons chopped green
   onions

Combine first 7 ingredients in container of a food processor or electric blender; top with cover, and process until blended. Spread mixture into a ½-inch-thick circle on a serving plate. Cover and refrigerate at least 8 hours.

Spread chutney over top, and sprinkle with 2 tablespoons green onions. Serve with crackers. Yield: about 1 cup.

Arugula, Endive, and Carrot Salad

1 head Belgian endive
2 medium carrots, scraped
4 cups torn arugula
¼ cup plus 1 tablespoon sugar
¼ cup vinegar
2 teaspoons Dijon mustard
½ teaspoon salt
¼ teaspoon dry mustard
½ cup plus 2 tablespoons
  vegetable oil

Cut off and discard bottom of endive. Separate leaves of endive; wash and pat dry. Cut each endive leaf into julienne strips; set aside. Using a vegetable peeler, apply firm pressure to carrots, and cut lengthwise into thin strips. Combine endive, carrot, and arugula; toss gently, and set aside.

Combine sugar and vinegar in a small saucepan. Place over low heat, and cook, stirring constantly, until sugar dissolves. Cool slightly. Place sugar mixture, Dijon mustard, salt, and dry mustard in container of an electric blender. Top with cover, and process 30 seconds. With blender running, add oil in a slow, steady stream. Process 30 seconds or until well blended. Drizzle dressing mixture over salad, and serve immediately. Yield: 4 servings.

Blackened Breast of Duck, Green Beans in Raspberry Vinaigrette, and Twice-Baked Potato Spirals can be arranged in an attractive pattern.

Blackened Breast of Duck

2 (4½-pound) dressed
  ducklings
¾ cup apricot preserves
¼ cup orange juice
¼ cup soy sauce
3 tablespoons honey
1 tablespoon prepared mustard
⅛ teaspoon garlic powder

Wash ducklings, and pat dry. Remove giblets and neck from ducklings; reserve for other uses, if desired. Remove legs, thighs, and wings from one duckling; reserve for other uses. Separate breast from back by cutting along each side of backbone between rib joints, using a sharp knife; reserve back for other uses, if desired.

Split breast into two lengthwise pieces by cutting along breastbone. Place duckling breast half on work surface, bone side down. Starting at the breastbone side, slice meat away from the bone, using a sharp knife. Repeat procedure with other duckling to make 4 boneless duck breast halves with skin on. Arrange breast halves in a large shallow pan.

Combine apricot preserves and remaining ingredients, stirring well. Pour apricot mixture over breast halves; cover and chill 30 minutes.

Place duck breast halves, skin side up, on grill. Grill over medium coals 5 minutes on each side or until skin is blackened but meat is pink. Slice each breast half into thin diagonal slices (the blackened portion should show on outer edges of slices). Arrange on serving plates. Yield: 4 servings.

Green Beans in Raspberry Vinaigrette

1 pound fresh green beans
½ cup vegetable oil
½ cup raspberry vinegar
2 tablespoons sugar
½ teaspoon salt
¼ teaspoon white pepper

Wash beans; trim ends, and remove strings. Arrange beans in a vegetable steamer, and place over boiling water; cover and steam 8 minutes or until crisp-tender. Plunge beans into ice water; drain well, and pat dry. Place beans in a large shallow container; set aside.

Combine oil, vinegar, sugar, salt, and pepper in a small saucepan. Cook over low heat, stirring constantly, until sugar dissolves. Let cool. Stir vinaigrette with a wire whisk, and pour over beans. Cover and chill 4 hours. Serve beans with a slotted spoon. Yield: 4 servings.

Twice-Baked Potato Spirals

4 medium-size baking potatoes
  (2 pounds)
Vegetable oil
2 egg yolks
3 tablespoons whipping cream
1 tablespoon butter or margarine,
  melted
1 tablespoon finely chopped
  fresh chives
½ teaspoon salt
¼ teaspoon white pepper
¼ teaspoon garlic powder
1 egg
1 tablespoon olive oil
Paprika (optional)

Wash potatoes, and rub with vegetable oil. Bake at 400° for 1 hour or until done. Let potatoes cool to touch. Cut potatoes in half lengthwise. Scoop out pulp; discard shells. Place pulp in a large bowl, and mash. Add egg yolks and next 6 ingredients; beat at medium speed of an electric mixer until smooth and blended (mixture will be stiff).

Lightly grease a large baking sheet. Spoon potato mixture into a decorating bag fitted with a No. 4B or 6B open star tip. Pipe potato mixture into eight 4- to 5-inch-long spiral shapes. Chill thoroughly.

Combine egg and olive oil, beating well. Brush potato spirals lightly with egg mixture, using a small, soft-bristled brush. Sprinkle with paprika, if desired. Bake at 400° for 25 to 30 minutes or until edges are lightly browned. Yield: 4 servings.

Pear Tart with Brandy Whip

1½ cups all-purpose flour
½ teaspoon baking powder
¼ teaspoon salt
⅓ cup shortening
3 tablespoons butter
3 tablespoons plus 1½ teaspoons
  milk
1 cup slivered blanched almonds
½ cup firmly packed brown sugar
1 egg
1 tablespoon butter, melted
⅔ cup water
¼ cup lemon juice
5 medium pears
2 tablespoons sugar
1 tablespoon plus 1½ teaspoons
  butter or margarine
1 tablespoon sugar
2 tablespoons peach preserves
1 tablespoon orange juice
2 teaspoons apricot brandy
1 cup whipping cream
2 tablespoons powdered sugar
1 tablespoon apricot brandy

Combine first 3 ingredients; cut in shortening and 3 tablespoons butter with a pastry blender until mixture resembles coarse meal. Sprinkle milk (1 tablespoon at a time) over surface; stir with a fork until dry ingredients are moistened. Shape into a ball; chill 1 hour.

Roll dough to ⅛-inch thickness on a lightly floured surface. Fit pastry in an 11-inch round tart pan with removable sides. Set aside.

Position knife blade in food processor bowl. Add almonds, and top with cover; process 40 to 50 seconds or until finely ground. Add brown sugar, egg, and 1 tablespoon melted butter. Top with cover; process until well mixed. Spread almond mixture evenly over bottom of pastry. Set aside.

Combine water and lemon juice; peel and core pears. Dip pears in lemon juice mixture; drain well. Cut pears in half vertically, and cut into ½-inch-thick lengthwise slices. Arrange pears so that slices are overlapping, curved side up, in rows on top of almond mixture. Sprinkle with 2 tablespoons sugar, and dot with 1 tablespoon plus 1½ teaspoons butter. Bake at 400° for 40 to 50 minutes or until golden brown.

Combine 1 tablespoon sugar, preserves, orange juice, and 2 teaspoons brandy in a small saucepan; cook over low heat, stirring constantly, until sugar dissolves. Press preserve mixture through a sieve, reserving syrup. Brush syrup over tart. Carefully remove sides of tart pan before serving.

Beat whipping cream until foamy; gradually add powdered sugar and 1 tablespoon brandy, beating until soft peaks form. Serve each slice of tart with a dollop of whipped cream. Yield: one 11-inch tart.

Pear Tart with Brandy Whip is the ultimate in fruit desserts. The flaky crust and sweet filling make it a winner.

Down by the River

One way to have lots of fun is to throw a fish fry right on the river bank. Hungry guests can fill up on plenty of good food—Curry Dip, Puffy Fried Catfish, Ice Water Onion Rings, Marinated Slaw, and Garden Hush Puppies. And don't forget to get out the ice cream churn and work up a batch of Peanut Butter Ice Cream. Serve all this with Cream Cheese Swirl Brownies, beer, and iced tea.

Down by the River

Curry Dip

Puffy Fried Catfish

Ice Water Onion Rings

Marinated Slaw

Garden Hush Puppies

Cream Cheese Swirl Brownies

Peanut Butter Ice Cream

Beer

Iced Tea

Serves eight

Curry Dip

2 cups mayonnaise
1 teaspoon garlic powder
1 teaspoon dry mustard
½ teaspoon curry powder
½ teaspoon celery seeds
¼ teaspoon instant minced onion
1½ teaspoons prepared horseradish
1 teaspoon white wine Worcestershire sauce
⅛ teaspoon hot sauce

Combine all ingredients in a medium bowl, and stir well. Cover dip, and chill thoroughly. Serve chilled dip with assorted fresh vegetables. Yield: 2 cups.

A dinner of Puffy Fried Catfish is sure to satisfy. The fish are cooked in deep, hot oil until golden on both sides.

Puffy Fried Catfish

8 whole catfish, cleaned and
    dressed (3½ to 4 pounds)
Lemon juice
2½ cups all-purpose flour, divided
2 teaspoons salt, divided
1 tablespoon paprika
1 (12-ounce) can beer
Vegetable oil
Sprigs of fresh parsley (optional)
Lemon wedges (optional)

Rinse fish with cold water, and pat dry. Place fish in a large shallow container; sprinkle both sides generously with lemon juice. Cover and chill 20 minutes.

Combine 1¼ cups flour and 1 teaspoon salt, stirring well. Dredge fish in flour mixture; set fish aside.

Combine remaining 1¼ cups flour, remaining 1 teaspoon salt, and paprika. Add beer, and stir until smooth. Dip fish into batter. Fry in deep hot oil (375°) until fish float to the top and are golden brown on both sides. Drain on paper towels. If desired, garnish with fresh parsley sprigs and lemon wedges. Yield: 8 servings.

Ice Water Onion Rings

2 large Spanish onions (1½
    pounds)
1½ cups all-purpose flour
1 tablespoon plus 1½ teaspoons
    cornmeal
2 teaspoons baking powder
1½ teaspoons salt
¼ teaspoon pepper
1¼ cups milk
2 eggs, separated
1 tablespoon vegetable oil
Vegetable oil

Peel onions; cut into ¼-inch slices, and separate into rings. Place onion slices in a large bowl with ice water to cover. Cover and chill 30 minutes.

Combine flour and next 4 ingredients in a large bowl. Combine milk, egg yolks, and 1 tablespoon oil; beat well. Add to dry ingredients, mixing well. Beat egg whites (at room temperature) in a medium bowl at high speed of an electric mixer until stiff peaks form; fold beaten egg whites into batter.

Drain onion rings on paper towels. Dip onion rings in batter; fry in deep hot oil (375°) for 3 to 5 minutes or until golden brown. Drain on paper towels. Yield: 8 servings.

Marinated Slaw

1 medium cabbage, shredded
1 green pepper, finely chopped
1 medium onion, finely chopped
24 pimiento-stuffed olives, sliced
½ teaspoon salt
½ cup vinegar
½ cup vegetable oil
½ cup sugar
1 teaspoon celery seeds
½ teaspoon mustard seeds

Combine cabbage, green pepper, onion, olives, and salt in a large bowl; stir well, and set aside.

Combine vinegar, oil, sugar, celery seeds, and mustard seeds in a small saucepan; bring to a boil. Pour dressing mixture over vegetables, tossing gently. Cover and chill at least 8 hours. Yield: 8 servings.

Garden Hush Puppies

⅓ cup chopped tomato
1¼ cups commercial hush
  puppy mix
⅓ cup shredded yellow squash
⅓ cup beer
¼ cup chopped green pepper
2 green onions, chopped

1 egg, beaten
¼ teaspoon garlic salt
¼ teaspoon baking powder
¼ teaspoon crushed
  red pepper
¼ teaspoon pepper
Vegetable oil

Press tomato between paper towels to remove excess moisture. Combine tomato and next 10 ingredients in a medium bowl; stir well. Drop batter by tablespoonfuls into deep hot oil (375°); fry 3 to 5 minutes or until golden brown, turning once. Drain on paper towels. Yield: 1½ dozen.

Cream Cheese Swirl Brownies

1 (4-ounce) package sweet baking
  chocolate
¼ cup plus 1 tablespoon butter
  or margarine, divided
½ (8-ounce) package cream
  cheese, softened
¼ cup sifted powdered sugar
3 eggs, divided
1 tablespoon all-purpose flour

½ teaspoon vanilla extract
½ cup sugar
¼ cup firmly packed brown sugar
½ cup all-purpose flour
½ teaspoon baking powder
¼ teaspoon salt
1 tablespoon Kahlúa or other
  coffee-flavored liqueur

Melt chocolate and 3 tablespoons butter over low heat, stirring constantly. Set aside to cool.

Cream remaining 2 tablespoons butter and cream cheese in a medium bowl. Gradually add powdered sugar, mixing until light and fluffy. Stir in 1 egg, 1 tablespoon flour, and vanilla. Set aside.

Beat remaining 2 eggs at medium speed of an electric mixer until thick and lemon colored. Gradually add ½ cup sugar and brown sugar, beating until thickened. Combine ½ cup flour, baking powder, and salt; add to egg mixture, mixing well. Stir in cooled chocolate mixture and liqueur.

Spread half of chocolate batter in a greased 8-inch square baking pan. Spoon cream cheese mixture over chocolate batter; top with remaining chocolate batter. Swirl batter with a knife to create a marble effect. Bake at 350° for 35 to 40 minutes. Cool; cut into 2-inch squares. Yield: 16 brownies.

Peanut Butter Ice Cream

4 cups milk
4 eggs
2 cups sugar
1 cup creamy peanut butter
4 cups half-and-half
2 cups whipping cream
½ cup chopped roasted peanuts
1 teaspoon salt
2 teaspoons vanilla extract

Place milk in top of a double boiler; bring water to a boil. Reduce heat to low, and cook until milk is thoroughly heated. Set aside.

Beat eggs at medium speed of an electric mixer until frothy. Gradually add sugar, beating until thickened. Gradually stir about one-fourth of hot milk into egg mixture; add to remaining hot milk, stirring constantly. Cook custard mixture in top of double boiler over low heat, stirring frequently, until mixture begins to thicken. Remove from heat, and stir in peanut butter. Cool 15 minutes; chill at least 2 hours.

Pour chilled custard into freezer can of a 5-quart hand-turned or electric freezer. Add half-and-half, whipping cream, chopped peanuts, salt, and vanilla, stirring well. Freeze according to manufacturer's instructions. Let ripen at least 1½ hours before serving. Yield: 4 quarts.

No fancy presentation is needed for Peanut Butter Ice Cream and Cream Cheese Swirl Brownies; they will taste delicious no matter how they are served.

Scenic Tailgating

Tailgating doesn't have to be reserved for football games. Why not journey to a lovely scenic location and unload this stylish feast? Spread out a pretty rug, light the candelabra, and chill a crisp, white wine. What a way to enjoy Tomato-Phyllo Appetizers, Roasted Red Pepper Salad, Grilled Shrimp Kabobs, Minted Orange Rice, and Sweet Glazed Baby Brussels Sprouts. A slice of Lime Cheesecake and a cup of hot coffee will help you enjoy the view.

Scenic Tailgating

Tomato-Phyllo Appetizers

Roasted Red Pepper Salad

Grilled Shrimp Kabobs

Minted Orange Rice

Sweet Glazed Baby Brussels Sprouts

Saint-Véran-Georges Duboeuf

Lime Cheesecake

Coffee

Serves six

Tomato-Phyllo Appetizers

2 sheets commercial frozen
  phyllo pastry, thawed
3 to 4 tablespoons butter or
  margarine, melted
½ cup (2 ounces) shredded
  Monterey Jack cheese, divided
1 cup diced tomato, drained
1½ teaspoons mayonnaise
1½ teaspoons Dijon mustard
1 to 2 tablespoons minced fresh
  parsley

Place 1 sheet of phyllo on a damp towel (keep remaining phyllo covered). Lightly brush phyllo with melted butter. Place remaining sheet of phyllo on first sheet; brush with melted butter. Fold phyllo in half lengthwise, making 4 layers; cut into twelve 3-inch squares, using kitchen shears.

Brush miniature (1¾-inch) muffin cups with melted butter. Place one square of layered phyllo in each muffin cup, pressing gently in center to form a pastry cup. Bake at 350° for 8 to 10 minutes or until golden.

Sprinkle ¼ cup cheese in pastry cups. Press tomato between paper towels to remove excess moisture. Combine tomato, mayonnaise, and mustard; stir gently, and spoon into pastry cups. Top with remaining ¼ cup cheese. Bake at 350° for 2 minutes or until cheese melts. Sprinkle with parsley. Yield: 1 dozen.

Each bite of Tomato-Phyllo Appetizers is filled with cheese, tomato, mayonnaise, mustard, and crisp pastry.

Roasted Red Pepper Salad

3 medium-size sweet red peppers
¼ cup extra-virgin olive oil
3 cups torn arugula
3 cups torn leaf lettuce
⅓ cup red wine vinegar
2 cloves garlic, minced
¼ teaspoon salt
½ teaspoon coarsely ground
   pepper
⅔ cup extra-virgin olive oil
1 cup grated fontina cheese

Wash and dry peppers. Cut peppers in half lengthwise, removing seeds. Place peppers, skin side up, on a baking sheet. Broil 6 inches from heat 5 to 10 minutes or until skins are charred. Place peppers in a plastic bag; seal tightly, and let stand 10 minutes. Remove and discard skins. Cut peppers into ½-inch-wide strips. Combine pepper strips and ¼ cup olive oil; set aside.

Combine torn arugula and lettuce in a large bowl; toss well. Combine vinegar, garlic, salt, and pepper in a small bowl. Gradually add ⅔ cup olive oil in a slow, steady stream, stirring with a wire whisk.

Before serving, drain peppers, and add to greens; top with vinegar mixture, and toss gently. Sprinkle cheese evenly over top. Serve immediately. Yield: 6 servings.

Grilled Shrimp Kabobs

1 medium onion, diced
4 cloves garlic, minced
½ cup vegetable oil
¼ cup plus 2 tablespoons lemon juice
3 tablespoons soy sauce
2 teaspoons ground ginger
2 pounds unpeeled jumbo fresh shrimp (about 3 dozen)

Combine first 6 ingredients in a large shallow dish; stir well. Peel shrimp; add shrimp to marinade mixture in shallow dish, tossing gently to coat. Cover and marinate in refrigerator at least 2 hours.

Remove shrimp from marinade. Thread tail and neck of each shrimp onto six 14-inch metal skewers (arrange shrimp to lie flat). Grill over medium-hot coals 3 to 4 minutes on each side or until shrimp turn pink. Yield: 6 servings.

Minted Orange Rice

1¾ cups plus 2 tablespoons orange juice
1¾ cups plus 2 tablespoons water
2 tablespoons minced fresh mint leaves
1 tablespoon plus 1½ teaspoons butter or margarine
1½ teaspoons chicken-flavored bouillon granules
¾ teaspoon salt
1½ cups uncooked long-grain rice

Combine orange juice, water, mint, butter, bouillon granules, and salt in a saucepan; bring to a boil. Stir in rice; cover, reduce heat, and simmer 20 minutes or until liquid is absorbed. Yield: 6 servings.

Sweet Glazed Baby Brussels Sprouts

1½ pounds baby brussels sprouts
½ cup water
¼ cup firmly packed brown sugar
3 tablespoons butter or margarine
3 tablespoons water
½ teaspoon grated lemon rind
¼ teaspoon salt

Wash brussels sprouts thoroughly, and remove discolored leaves. Cut off stem ends, and slash bottom of each sprout with a shallow x. Bring ½ cup water to a boil in a large saucepan; add brussels sprouts. Cover, reduce heat, and simmer 6 to 8 minutes or until sprouts are crisp-tender; drain and set aside.

Combine brown sugar and remaining ingredients in a large skillet; bring to a boil, stirring constantly. Reduce heat, and simmer, uncovered, 5 minutes, stirring constantly. Add brussels sprouts, and cook over medium heat 5 minutes, stirring frequently. Serve with a slotted spoon. Yield: 6 servings.

Lime Cheesecake

1¼ cups graham cracker crumbs
2 tablespoons sugar
¼ cup butter or margarine, melted
1 teaspoon grated lime rind
3 (8-ounce) packages cream cheese, softened
¾ cup sugar
3 eggs
1 tablespoon grated lime rind
¼ cup Key lime juice
1 teaspoon vanilla extract
2 cups sour cream
3 tablespoons sugar
Fresh strawberries (optional)
Lime slices (optional)

Combine first 4 ingredients; stir well. Press crumb mixture evenly over bottom and up sides of a 9-inch springform pan. Bake at 350° for 5 to 6 minutes. Let cool.

Beat cream cheese until light and fluffy; gradually add ¾ cup sugar, beating well. Add eggs, one at a time, beating well after each addition. Stir in lime rind, juice, and vanilla. Pour mixture into prepared pan. Bake at 375° for 45 minutes or until set.

Combine sour cream and 3 tablespoons sugar; stir well, and spread evenly over cheesecake. Bake at 500° for 5 minutes. Let cool to room temperature on a wire rack; chill at least 8 hours. To serve, carefully remove sides of springform pan. If desired, garnish with strawberries and lime slices. Yield: one 9-inch cheesecake.

If you are a connoisseur of Key lime pie, you will love Lime Cheesecake. It is thick, rich, and has just the right amount of tangy lime flavor.

Lakeside Picnic at Dusk

A tranquil spot on the edge of the lake invites a long, lingering meal and plenty of good conversation. Serve Barbecued Cashews, Shrimp Salad in Pepper Cups, Marinated Mushrooms, Stuffed Celery Sticks, Pickled Okra, Cheese Biscuits, and a flowery, semi-dry white wine. End this idyllic meal with a slice of Lemon Loaf Pound Cake.

205

Lakeside Picnic at Dusk

Barbecued Cashews

———

Shrimp Salad in Pepper Cups

Marinated Mushrooms

Stuffed Celery Sticks

Pickled Okra

Cheese Biscuits

Joseph Phelps Johannisberg Riesling

———

Lemon Loaf Pound Cake

———

Water

Serves four

Barbecued Cashews

2 tablespoons butter or margarine
1 tablespoon white wine Worcestershire sauce
1 tablespoon plus 1 teaspoon soy sauce
1 teaspoon hot sauce
½ teaspoon salt
¼ teaspoon chili powder
¼ teaspoon ground red pepper
2 cups cashews

Melt butter in a large saucepan. Remove from heat; add Worcestershire sauce, soy sauce, hot sauce, salt, chili powder, and red pepper, stirring well. Add cashews, stirring to coat well.

Spread cashews in an aluminum foil-lined 15- x 10- x 1-inch jellyroll pan. Bake at 350° for 10 to 15 minutes, stirring every 5 minutes. Place cashews on paper towels, and cool completely. Yield: 2 cups.

Guests will want to linger over Shrimp Salad in Pepper Cups and Stuffed Celery Sticks; they are crisp and colorful.

Shrimp Salad in Pepper Cups

6 cups water
2 pounds unpeeled medium-size
   fresh shrimp
½ cup pimiento-stuffed olives
½ cup finely chopped green
   pepper
2 tablespoons chopped sweet
   pickle
2 tablespoons chopped green
   onions
1 cup commercial creamy
   buttermilk salad dressing
4 large sweet red or yellow
   peppers

Bring water to a boil; add shrimp, and cook 3 to 5 minutes. Drain well; rinse shrimp with cold water. Chill. Peel shrimp.

Combine olives, green pepper, pickle, onions, and salad dressing in a large bowl, stirring well. Stir in shrimp. Cut off tops of peppers; remove seeds. Spoon shrimp mixture into pepper cups. Yield: 4 servings.

Marinated Mushrooms

1 pound medium-size fresh
   mushrooms
¾ cup commercial Italian salad
   dressing
½ teaspoon dried parsley flakes
½ teaspoon dried whole basil
¼ teaspoon onion salt
¼ teaspoon dried whole
   dillweed

Clean mushrooms with damp paper towels. Combine mushrooms and remaining ingredients, tossing gently. Cover and chill at least 4 hours. Serve, using a slotted spoon. Yield: 4 cups.

Stuffed Celery Sticks

1 (3-ounce) package cream
   cheese, softened
⅓ cup finely chopped toasted
   pecans
2 tablespoons mayonnaise
1 tablespoon dried parsley flakes
¼ teaspoon Beau Monde
   seasoning
⅛ teaspoon garlic powder
4 celery stalks, cut into 3-inch
   pieces

Combine first 6 ingredients; mix well. Spread onto celery pieces. Cover and chill at least 4 hours. Yield: 1 dozen.

Pickled Okra

2½ to 3 pounds small okra pods
12 cloves garlic
6 fresh small hot peppers
6 fresh dillweed sprigs
1 tablespoon dillseeds
1 quart water
2 cups vinegar (5% acidity)
⅓ cup pickling salt

Pack okra tightly into hot sterilized jars, leaving ½-inch headspace; place 2 garlic cloves, 1 hot pepper, 1 dillweed sprig, and ½ teaspoon dillseeds in each jar with okra.

Combine water, vinegar, and pickling salt in a large saucepan; bring to a boil. Pour boiling vinegar mixture over okra, leaving ½-inch headspace. Remove air bubbles; wipe jar rims. Cover at once with metal lids, and screw on bands. Process in boiling-water bath 10 minutes. Yield: 6 pints.

Cheese Biscuits

1 cup all-purpose flour
1½ teaspoons baking powder
⅛ teaspoon salt
¼ cup shortening
½ cup (2 ounces) shredded sharp Cheddar cheese
¼ cup milk

Combine flour, baking powder, and salt in a medium bowl; cut in shortening and cheese with a pastry blender until mixture resembles coarse meal. Add milk, stirring until dry ingredients are moistened. Turn dough out onto a lightly floured surface, and knead lightly 3 or 4 times.

Roll dough to ½-inch thickness; cut into rounds with a 2¼-inch biscuit cutter. Place biscuits on a lightly greased baking sheet. Bake at 450° for 10 to 12 minutes or until golden. Yield: 8 biscuits.

Lemon Loaf Pound Cake

¼ cup butter or margarine, softened
¼ cup shortening
1 cup sugar
2 eggs
¼ teaspoon baking soda
1½ teaspoons lemon juice
½ cup milk
1½ cups all-purpose flour
⅛ teaspoon salt
1½ teaspoons lemon extract

Cream butter and shortening; gradually add sugar, beating well at medium speed of an electric mixer. Add eggs, one at a time, beating after each addition.

Combine soda, lemon juice, and milk; let stand 1 minute or until soda dissolves. Combine flour and salt; add to creamed mixture alternately with milk mixture, beginning and ending with flour mixture. Mix just until blended after each addition. Stir in lemon extract.

Pour batter into a greased and floured 8½- x 4½- x 3-inch loafpan. Bake at 350° for 55 to 60 minutes or until a wooden pick inserted in center comes out clean. Cool in pan 10 to 15 minutes; remove from pan, and let cool completely on a wire rack. Yield: one 8-inch loaf.

Pickled Okra, Cheese Biscuits, and Lemon Loaf Pound Cake are traditional Southern comfort foods.

Beside a
Garden Pond

This shady courtyard provides a peaceful, inviting spot to enjoy Best Crab Spread with a semisweet white wine. As you listen to the gently flowing fountain, savor Gingered Hearts of Palm Salad, Grilled Pork Tenderloin and Pineapple, Citrus Rice, Sesame Snow Peas, and Refrigerator Yeast Rolls. And if you share an enthusiasm for tart Lemon Meringue Pie, you will agree that this one is the best you have ever had.

211

Beside a
Garden Pond

Best Crab Spread

Vouvray-Marc Brédif

Gingered Hearts of Palm Salad

Grilled Pork Tenderloin and Pineapple

Citrus Rice

Sesame Snow Peas

Refrigerator Yeast Rolls

Lemon Meringue Pie

Water

Serves six

Best Crab Spread

½ (8-ounce) package cream
  cheese, softened
¼ cup mayonnaise
1 tablespoon honey mustard
1 tablespoon lemon juice
1 pound fresh lump crabmeat,
  drained
3 tablespoons minced celery
3 tablespoons minced green
  onions
⅛ teaspoon white pepper
⅛ teaspoon hot sauce
Radish slices (optional)
Lemon wedges (optional)
Sprigs of fresh chives (optional)

Combine first 4 ingredients in a
mixing bowl; beat at medium speed
of an electric mixer until smooth.
Stir in crabmeat, celery, green
onions, pepper, and hot sauce. If
desired, garnish with radish slices,
lemon wedges, and chives. Serve
with assorted crackers. Yield: about
2½ cups.

*Best Crab Spread looks pretty garnished
with radish slices and lemon wedges.*

Gingered Hearts of Palm Salad is filled with interesting textures and flavors. The dressing is a surprise—it is lightly flavored with peanut butter.

Gingered Hearts of Palm Salad

¼ cup plus 2 tablespoons
  whipping cream
3 tablespoons mayonnaise
3 tablespoons creamy peanut
  butter
2 tablespoons plus 1 teaspoon
  orange juice
2 heads Bibb lettuce
1 (14.4-ounce) can hearts of
  palm, drained and sliced
¾ cup sliced strawberries
¾ cup mandarin oranges, drained
½ cup chopped celery
3 tablespoons golden raisins
2 tablespoons finely chopped
  crystallized ginger

Combine first 4 ingredients in a small bowl, stirring well. Cover and chill thoroughly.

Wash lettuce, and separate into leaves. Place lettuce on individual salad plates. Arrange hearts of palm, strawberries, orange sections, celery, and raisins evenly over each salad. Drizzle chilled dressing over salads. Sprinkle with ginger. Yield: 6 servings.

Grilled Pork Tenderloin and Pineapple

3 tablespoons soy sauce
2 tablespoons lime juice
2 tablespoons orange juice
2 tablespoons vegetable oil
2 tablespoons minced fresh
  gingerroot
½ teaspoon dry mustard
¼ teaspoon garlic powder
2 (1-pound) pork tenderloins
6 (½-inch-thick) slices fresh
  pineapple

Combine first 7 ingredients in a small bowl; stir well. Trim excess fat from tenderloins. Place tenderloins in a large, shallow dish. Pour marinade mixture over tenderloins. Cover and marinate in refrigerator 24 hours, turning occasionally.

Remove tenderloins from marinade, reserving marinade. Pour marinade into a small saucepan. Cook over low heat just until thoroughly heated; set marinade aside. Insert meat thermometer into thickest part of tenderloin, making sure it does not touch fat. Grill tenderloins over medium coals 45 minutes or until meat thermometer registers 160°, turning and basting frequently with reserved marinade. Grill pineapple slices for 5 minutes or until browned on both sides. Cut pineapple slices in half crosswise. Slice tenderloins, and serve with pineapple. Yield: 6 servings.

Citrus Rice

2 teaspoons butter or margarine
⅓ cup thinly sliced celery
¼ cup chopped green onions
½ cup orange juice
1 tablespoon grated lemon rind
2 cups water
½ teaspoon salt
1 cup uncooked long-grain rice
Lemon rind curl (optional)

Melt butter in a large skillet; add celery and green onions, and sauté until crisp-tender.

Stir in orange juice, grated lemon rind, water, and salt; bring mixture to a boil. Stir in rice. Cover, reduce heat, and simmer 20 minutes or until rice is tender and liquid is absorbed. Garnish with a lemon rind curl, if desired. Yield: 6 servings.

Grilled Pork Tenderloin and Pineapple can be arranged with Citrus Rice and Sesame Snow Peas for a striking presentation.

Sesame Snow Peas

1 pound fresh snow pea pods
½ cup water
1 tablespoon light sesame oil
1 tablespoon sesame seeds,
  toasted
1 tablespoon lemon juice
¼ teaspoon white pepper
⅛ teaspoon salt

Trim ends and stems from snow peas. Place water in a saucepan; bring to a boil. Add peas; cover, reduce heat, and simmer 3 to 5 minutes or until crisp-tender. Drain; plunge peas into cold water. Drain again; pat dry with paper towels.

Heat sesame oil in a large skillet; add peas, and cook, stirring constantly, just until heated. Sprinkle with sesame seeds, lemon juice, pepper, and salt, tossing well. Serve immediately. Yield: 6 servings.

Refrigerator Yeast Rolls

2½ to 3 cups all-purpose flour,
  divided
1 package dry yeast
¼ cup sugar
½ teaspoon salt
¼ cup water
¼ cup milk
¼ cup butter or margarine
2 eggs
3 tablespoons butter or
  margarine, melted

Combine 1½ cups flour, yeast, sugar, and salt in a large bowl; stir well. Combine water, milk, and ¼ cup butter in a small saucepan. Heat until butter melts, stirring occasionally. Cool to 120° to 130°.

Gradually add milk mixture and eggs to flour mixture. Beat at medium speed of an electric mixer 3 minutes. Gradually stir in enough remaining flour to make a soft dough (dough will be sticky). Cover tightly, and refrigerate 8 to 12 hours.

Divide dough in half; divide each half into thirds. Divide each third into 6 pieces; shape each piece into a smooth ball. Dip each ball in melted butter. Place 3 balls in each cup of a lightly greased muffin pan. Cover and let rise in a warm place (85°), free from drafts, 15 to 20 minutes or until dough is almost doubled in bulk. Bake at 400° for 8 to 10 minutes. Yield: 1 dozen.

Lemon Meringue Pie

1¼ cups sugar
½ cup cornstarch
¼ teaspoon salt
1½ cups cold water
4 eggs, separated
1 tablespoon butter or margarine
¼ cup plus 2 tablespoons lemon
  juice
2 teaspoons grated lemon rind
1 baked 9-inch pastry shell
½ teaspoon cream of tartar
¼ cup plus 2 tablespoons sugar

Combine 1¼ cups sugar, cornstarch, and salt in a heavy saucepan; stir well. Gradually add cold water, stirring until smooth. Cook over medium heat until mixture comes to a boil, stirring constantly. Boil 1 minute or until thickened.

Beat egg yolks until thick and lemon colored; remove cornstarch mixture from heat, and gradually stir about ½ cup hot cornstarch mixture into yolks. Add to remaining hot mixture, stirring constantly. Return pan to heat, and add butter; cook over medium-low heat, stirring constantly, 1 to 2 minutes or just until thickened (do not boil). Remove from heat, and stir in lemon juice and rind. Pour into pastry shell.

Beat egg whites (at room temperature) and cream of tartar at high speed of an electric mixer 1 minute. Gradually add ¼ cup plus 2 tablespoons sugar, 1 tablespoon at a time, beating until stiff peaks form and sugar dissolves (about 2 minutes). Spread meringue over hot filling, sealing to edge of pastry. Bake at 350° for 12 to 15 minutes or until golden brown. Let cool. Refrigerate at least 1 hour before serving. Yield: one 9-inch pie.

Picnic by a Stream

When you want to get away from it all, pack up a blanket and go on a picnic. Take along Herbed Cheese, Fancy Deviled Eggs, Bread and Butter Pickles, Cucumber-Salmon-Watercress Sandwiches, Sweet Shredded Carrots, and Marinated Vegetables. Rich Brownie Cupcakes, slices of watermelon, and glasses of sparkling white wine make quite a spread.

Picnic by a Stream

Herbed Cheese

Fancy Deviled Eggs

Bread and Butter Pickles

Cucumber-Salmon-Watercress
Sandwiches

Sweet Shredded Carrots

Marinated Vegetables

———————

Rich Brownie Cupcakes

Watermelon

———————

Domaine Cheurlin Brut

Serves six

Herbed Cheese

1 (8-ounce) package cream
  cheese, softened
1 (3-ounce) package cream
  cheese, softened
1½ teaspoons chopped fresh
  chives
1¼ teaspoons dried whole
  basil
1 teaspoon caraway seeds
1 teaspoon dillseeds
1 clove garlic, crushed
Lemon-pepper seasoning

Combine softened cream cheese, chives, basil, caraway seeds, dillseeds, and garlic in a medium bowl; stir well. Chill mixture until firm.

Shape into a 7-inch round patty, and coat evenly with lemon-pepper seasoning. Cover and chill at least 8 hours. Serve with assorted crackers. Yield: 1⅓ cups.

Fancy Deviled Eggs

6 hard-cooked eggs
3 tablespoons mayonnaise
1 tablespoon sweet pickle relish
1 teaspoon Dijon mustard
⅛ teaspoon salt
⅛ teaspoon white pepper
⅛ teaspoon curry powder
Tiny fresh marjoram leaves
Sprigs of fresh parsley

Slice eggs in half lengthwise, and carefully remove yolks; set egg whites aside.

Position knife blade in food processor bowl; add egg yolks, mayonnaise, pickle relish, Dijon mustard, salt, pepper, and curry powder. Top with cover, and process until mixture is smooth.

Spoon yolk mixture into a decorating bag fitted with a large tip. Pipe mixture into reserved egg whites. Garnish halves with tiny marjoram leaves. Serve eggs on a tray lined with parsley. Yield: 6 servings.

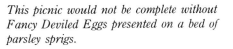

This picnic would not be complete without Fancy Deviled Eggs presented on a bed of parsley sprigs.

Bread and Butter Pickles

2½ pounds medium cucumbers, cut into ⅛-inch slices
3 medium onions, thinly sliced
¼ cup salt
2 cups vinegar (5% acidity)
1½ cups sugar
2 teaspoons celery seeds
1 teaspoon mustard seeds
1 teaspoon ground ginger

Layer cucumber, onion, and salt in a large container. Cover with ice. Let stand 2 hours. Drain and rinse thoroughly; drain again.

Combine vinegar and remaining ingredients in a large Dutch oven. Bring to a boil; add cucumber and onion. Reduce heat, and simmer, uncovered, 20 to 30 minutes or until tender.

Pack hot pickles into hot sterilized jars, leaving ½-inch headspace. Pour boiling syrup over pickles, leaving ½-inch headspace. Remove air bubbles; wipe jar rims. Cover at once with metal lids, and screw on bands. Process in boiling-water bath 10 minutes. Yield: 4 pints.

Cucumber-Salmon-Watercress Sandwiches

½ (8-ounce) package cream
    cheese, softened
3 tablespoons finely chopped
    cucumber
3 ounces smoked Nova Scotia
    salmon, thinly sliced
1 teaspoon minced watercress
    leaves
½ teaspoon lemon juice
⅛ teaspoon salt
⅛ teaspoon ground red pepper
12 slices whole wheat sandwich
    bread
3 tablespoons butter or
    margarine, softened
½ cup minced watercress leaves

Position knife blade in food processor bowl; add cream cheese. Top with cover, and process 8 to 10 seconds or until smooth. Add cucumber and next 5 ingredients; process until well blended.

Remove crust from bread slices. Cut bread into circles, using a large biscuit cutter, if desired. Spread filling on half the slices. Top with remaining slices. Carefully spread the cut outer edges of sandwiches with butter. Dip edges in ½ cup minced watercress to coat. Cover and refrigerate. Yield: 6 servings.

Here is a new twist to an old favorite—a chocolaty brownie recipe turned into Rich Brownie Cupcakes; they are just right for taking on a picnic.

Sweet Shredded Carrots

2 cups shredded carrots
¾ cup flaked coconut
¼ cup golden raisins
½ cup mandarin oranges, drained
½ cup pineapple tidbits, drained
½ cup sour cream

Combine first 3 ingredients, stirring well. Pat oranges and pineapple with paper towels to remove excess moisture; add to carrot mixture, stirring gently. Chill 45 minutes. Stir in sour cream. Yield: 6 servings.

Marinated Vegetables

1¼ cups thinly sliced carrots
1¼ cups thinly sliced yellow squash
1¼ cups broccoli flowerets
1¼ cups thinly sliced zucchini
¼ cup plus 2 tablespoons lemon juice
¼ cup plus 2 tablespoons vegetable oil
1 tablespoon plus 1 teaspoon sugar
½ teaspoon dried whole oregano
½ teaspoon salt
¼ teaspoon pepper
6 medium-size yellow peppers

Combine carrot, squash, broccoli, and zucchini in a shallow container. Combine lemon juice and next 5 ingredients, stirring well. Pour marinade mixture over vegetables, and toss gently. Cover and chill at least 8 hours. Cut off tops of yellow peppers; remove seeds. Cook peppers 5 minutes in boiling water to cover; drain and let cool. Fill with vegetable mixture. Yield: 6 servings.

Rich Brownie Cupcakes

¾ cup butter or margarine
2 (1-ounce) squares semisweet chocolate
1 (1-ounce) square unsweetened chocolate
1¾ cups sugar
4 eggs
1 teaspoon vanilla extract
1 cup all-purpose flour
2 tablespoons Dutch process cocoa
⅛ teaspoon salt
1 cup chopped pecans, toasted

Place butter and chocolate in a heavy saucepan; cook over low heat, stirring constantly, until melted. Remove from heat; stir in sugar. Add eggs, one at a time, stirring well after each addition; stir in vanilla. Combine flour, cocoa, and salt; add to chocolate mixture, stirring with a wire whisk until smooth. Stir in pecans. Spoon batter into paper-lined muffin pans, filling three-fourths full. Bake at 350° for 35 minutes. Yield: 16 cupcakes.

A Country Breakfast

Overnight guests will like getting up to this hearty breakfast. Screwdriver Twists and Festive Bloody Marys are sure to open sleepy eyes. And everyone will take pleasure in starting the day with Southern Ambrosia, Farmer Omelets, Miniature Sausage Muffins, Honey Butter, and coffee.

223

A Country Breakfast

Screwdriver Twists

Festive Bloody Marys

Southern Ambrosia

Farmer Omelets

Miniature Sausage Muffins

Honey Butter

Coffee

Water

Serves four

Screwdriver Twists

3½ cups orange juice
½ cup vodka
2 teaspoons lemon juice
2 teaspoons Triple Sec or other
   orange-flavored liqueur
Orange slices (optional)

Combine orange juice, vodka, lemon juice, and liqueur; stir well and chill. Serve over ice; garnish with orange slices, if desired. Yield: 4 cups.

Festive Bloody Marys

4½ cups tomato juice
¼ cup lime juice
3 tablespoons white wine
   Worcestershire sauce
1 teaspoon celery salt
1 teaspoon lemon-pepper
   seasoning
½ teaspoon coarsely ground
   pepper
¼ teaspoon hot sauce
1 cup vodka
Celery stalks (optional)

Combine first 7 ingredients; stir well, and chill. Stir in vodka, and serve over ice. Garnish each serving with a stalk of celery, if desired. Yield: 6 cups.

Start the morning on an agreeable note by offering Screwdriver Twists and Festive Bloody Marys.

Chopped green pepper, pimiento, green onions, and basil fill puffy Farmer Omelets with garden flavor.

Southern Ambrosia

3 medium oranges, peeled
  and sliced crosswise
2 bananas, sliced
⅓ cup orange juice
3 tablespoons honey
1 tablespoon lemon juice
¼ cup flaked coconut
Maraschino cherry halves
  (optional)

Combine sliced oranges and bananas in a medium bowl; toss gently. Combine orange juice, honey, and lemon juice in a small bowl; stir well, and pour over fruit. Sprinkle with coconut. Cover and chill at least 1 hour. Garnish with cherries, if desired. Yield: 4 servings.

Farmer Omelets

1 cup chopped green pepper
⅔ cup chopped green onions
¼ cup sliced pimiento
2 tablespoons butter or
  margarine, melted
½ teaspoon dried whole basil
8 eggs, separated
¼ cup water
½ teaspoon salt
¼ teaspoon white pepper
¼ cup butter or margarine
Sprigs of fresh basil (optional)

Sauté chopped green pepper, green onions, and sliced pimiento in 2 tablespoons melted butter until tender; sprinkle with ½ teaspoon dried whole basil. Set vegetable mixture aside, and keep warm.

Beat 2 egg yolks in a small bowl until thick and lemon colored. Beat 2 egg whites (at room temperature) until foamy; add 1 tablespoon water, ⅛ teaspoon salt, and a dash of white pepper. Beat until stiff peaks form. Fold whites into yolks.

Heat an ovenproof 8-inch omelet pan or heavy skillet over medium heat until hot enough to sizzle a drop of water. Add 1 tablespoon butter, and rotate pan to coat bottom. Spread egg mixture in pan. Cook, uncovered, 2 minutes or until lightly browned. Bake at 325° for 2 to 5 minutes or until a knife inserted in center comes out clean. Loosen omelet with a spatula.

Spoon ¼ cup vegetable mixture over half of omelet; fold omelet in half, and gently slide onto a serving plate. Keep warm. Repeat procedure with remaining ingredients for three additional omelets. Garnish each with a sprig of fresh basil, if desired. Yield: 4 servings.

Miniature Sausage Muffins

½ pound bulk pork sausage
⅓ cup chopped green onions
1 (6-ounce) package biscuit mix
½ teaspoon dry mustard
¼ teaspoon ground red pepper
½ cup milk
½ cup (2 ounces) finely shredded
  Cheddar cheese

Combine sausage and green onions in a skillet; cook over medium heat until sausage is browned, stirring to crumble. Drain well.

Combine biscuit mix, dry mustard, and red pepper; add milk, stirring just until moistened. Stir in sausage mixture and cheese (mixture will be thick). Spoon into greased miniature (1¾-inch) muffin pans, filling two-thirds full. Bake at 400° for 12 to 14 minutes or until muffins are golden. Remove from pans immediately; serve warm. Yield: about 2½ dozen.

Honey Butter

¼ cup plus 2 tablespoons butter,
  softened
⅔ cup honey
½ teaspoon grated lemon rind

Cream butter until light and fluffy; gradually add honey, beating well. Beat in lemon rind. Chill butter mixture several hours or overnight. Serve Honey Butter with muffins or toast. Yield: 1 cup.

Outdoor Spring Brunch

Wicker, lace, and flowers arranged in asparagus-lined
containers turn this spring brunch into a special occasion.
Greet guests with Mimosas before serving them sliced Soufflé
Roll with Red Pepper Filling, Dilled Ham Points,
Asparagus and Scallion Toss, and Marmalade Fruit Bake.
Baby Brioches and Cinnamon Coffee complete the menu.

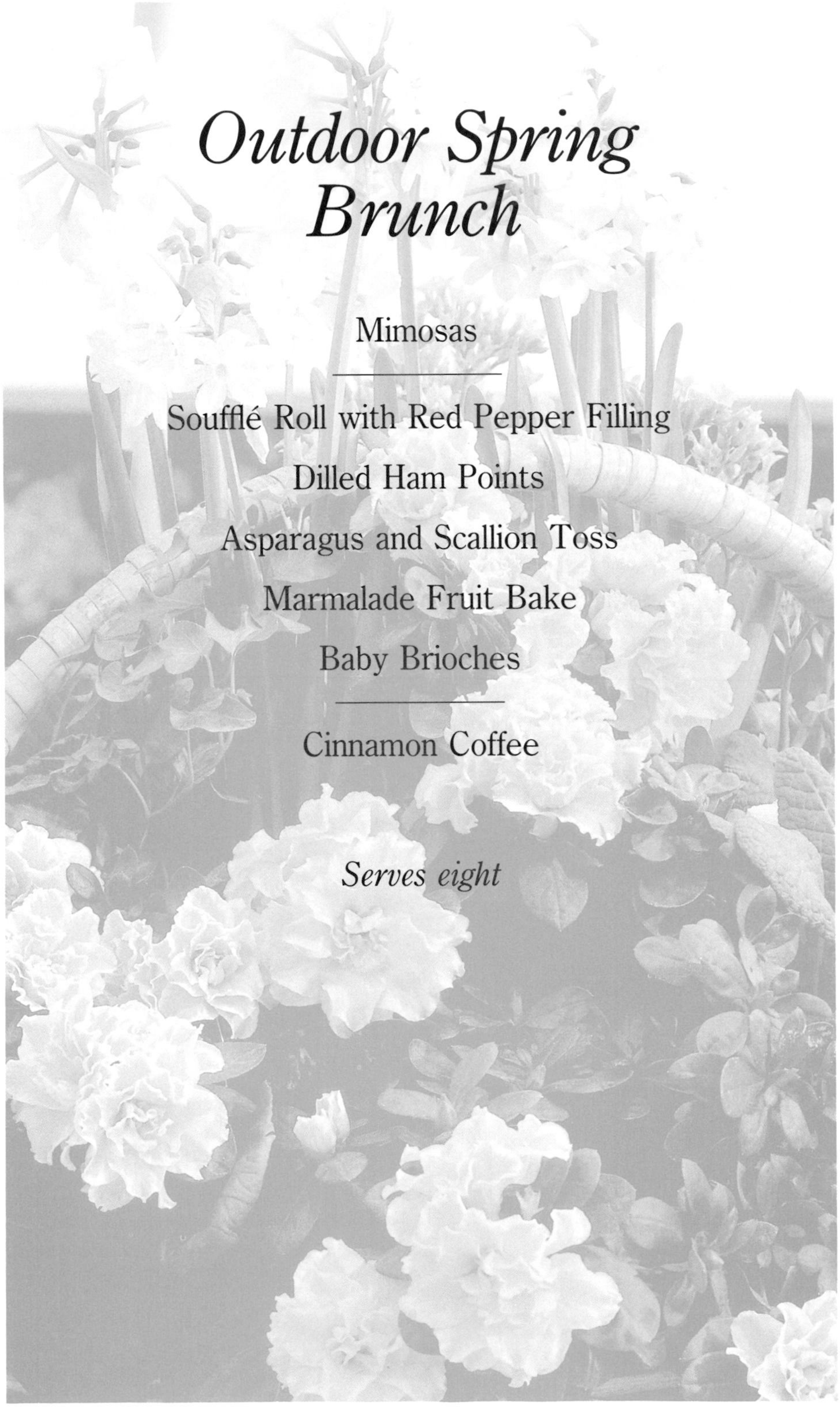

Outdoor Spring Brunch

Mimosas

Soufflé Roll with Red Pepper Filling

Dilled Ham Points

Asparagus and Scallion Toss

Marmalade Fruit Bake

Baby Brioches

Cinnamon Coffee

Serves eight

Mimosas

1 (12-ounce) can frozen orange
   juice concentrate, thawed and
   undiluted
¼ cup plus 2 tablespoons Triple
   Sec or other orange-flavored
   liqueur
1 (750-milliliter) bottle
   champagne, chilled

Prepare orange juice according to
can directions; stir in liqueur. Cover
and chill thoroughly. Stir in champagne just before serving. Yield:
about 2½ quarts.

Soufflé Roll with Red Pepper Filling

¼ cup plus 2 tablespoons
   all-purpose flour
¼ teaspoon garlic salt
⅓ cup butter or margarine
1 cup half-and-half
¼ cup milk
½ cup (2 ounces) shredded
   Cheddar cheese
2 tablespoons grated Parmesan
   cheese
6 eggs, separated
¾ teaspoon cream of tartar
¼ teaspoon salt
2 tablespoons grated Parmesan
   cheese
Red Pepper Filling

Grease a 15- x 10- x 1-inch jellyroll pan with vegetable oil. Set pan
aside. Combine flour and garlic salt
in a small bowl. Melt butter in a

large heavy saucepan over low heat; add flour mixture, and stir with a wire whisk. Cook 1 minute, stirring constantly. Gradually add half-and-half and milk; cook over medium heat, stirring constantly, until mixture thickens and leaves sides of pan. Remove from heat; beat in shredded Cheddar cheese and 2 tablespoons grated Parmesan cheese.

Beat egg yolks at high speed of an electric mixer until thick and lemon colored. Gradually stir one-fourth of hot cheese mixture into egg yolks; add to remaining cheese mixture, beating well.

Combine egg whites (at room temperature) and cream of tartar in a large bowl. Beat at high speed of an electric mixer until foamy. Add salt, and beat until stiff peaks form. Fold one-third of egg whites into cheese mixture. Carefully fold in remaining egg whites.

Pour soufflé mixture into prepared pan, spreading evenly. Bake at 350° for 15 to 20 minutes or until puffed and lightly browned. Loosen edges of soufflé with a metal spatula. Let soufflé cool 15 minutes in pan on a wire rack.

Turn soufflé out onto a double layer of wax paper sprinkled with 2 tablespoons Parmesan cheese. Spoon chilled Red Pepper Filling evenly over soufflé. Starting at long side and using wax paper for support, carefully roll soufflé, jellyroll fashion. Carefully slide roll, seam side down, onto a large serving platter. Yield: 8 servings.

Soufflé Roll with Red Pepper Filling is the star of this menu. It tastes delicious when accompanied by Dilled Ham Points and Asparagus and Scallion Toss.

Red Pepper Filling

2 cups chopped sweet red pepper
3 tablespoons chopped onion
1 tablespoon butter or margarine, melted
¾ cup (3 ounces) shredded Cheddar cheese
2 tablespoons sour cream
2 tablespoons grated Parmesan cheese
¼ teaspoon salt
¼ teaspoon dried whole basil

Sauté pepper and onion in butter in a large skillet until tender. Remove from heat. Position knife blade in food processor bowl; add pepper mixture. Top with cover, and process until pureed. Add cheddar cheese and remaining ingredients. Pulse 3 or 4 times or until well blended. Spoon mixture into a small bowl, and chill thoroughly. Yield: 1½ cups.

Dilled Ham Points

8 slices white bread
½ pound thinly sliced baked ham
¼ cup unsalted butter, softened
1 (3-ounce) package cream
   cheese, softened
1 teaspoon minced fresh dillweed
½ teaspoon dry mustard
Sprigs of fresh dillweed

Remove crust from bread; cut each slice in half diagonally. Toast bread triangles, and set aside.

Position knife blade in food processor bowl. Add ham, reserving 1 slice for garnish. Add butter, cream cheese, minced dillweed, and mustard. Top with cover, and process until smooth.

Spread ham mixture on toast triangles. Garnish each serving with a small piece of ham and a sprig of dillweed. Serve immediately. Yield: 8 servings.

Asparagus and Scallion Toss

2 pounds fresh asparagus
8 green onions, diagonally sliced
8 radishes, thinly sliced
¼ cup wine vinegar
¼ cup olive oil
½ teaspoon dried whole thyme
½ teaspoon dried whole basil
¼ teaspoon salt
¼ teaspoon white pepper

Snap off tough ends of asparagus. Remove scales from stalks with a knife or vegetable peeler, if desired. Cut spears diagonally into 1½-inch pieces. Cook asparagus, covered, in a small amount of boiling water 6 minutes or until crisp-tender; drain. Place asparagus in a large bowl; cover and chill thoroughly. Add green onions and radishes to asparagus; set aside.

Combine vinegar and remaining ingredients in a small jar; cover tightly, and shake until combined. Pour over vegetable mixture; toss gently before serving. Yield: 8 servings.

Marmalade Fruit Bake

¾ cup orange marmalade
½ cup orange juice
1½ teaspoons minced fresh
   mint leaves
2 (16-ounce) cans pear halves,
   drained
2 (16-ounce) cans peach halves,
   drained
1 (11-ounce) can mandarin
   oranges, drained
Sprigs of fresh mint (optional)
Orange twists (optional)

Combine marmalade, orange juice, and minced mint leaves in a small bowl; stir well. Set aside.

Place fruit in a lightly greased 13- x 9- x 2-inch baking dish. Pour marmalade mixture over fruit. Bake at 325° for 20 minutes or until fruit is thoroughly heated. Spoon fruit and marmalade mixture into individual serving bowls; if desired, garnish with mint sprigs and orange twists. Serve warm. Yield: 8 servings.

Delicately textured Baby Brioches will melt in your mouth, and Marmalade Fruit Bake, a new twist on baked fruit, will sweeten your day.

Baby Brioches

4 cups all-purpose flour, divided
1 package dry yeast
3 tablespoons sugar
½ teaspoon salt
½ cup water
½ cup butter
4 eggs
1 egg yolk
1 tablespoon water

Combine 2 cups flour, yeast, sugar, and salt in a large mixing bowl; stir well.

Combine water and butter in a saucepan; heat until butter melts, stirring occasionally. Cool to 120° to 130°. Add liquid mixture to flour mixture, and beat at medium speed of an electric mixer 1 minute. Add 4 eggs; beat until mixture is smooth. Gradually stir in remaining 2 cups flour (dough will be sticky).

Place dough in a well-greased bowl, turning to grease top. Cover and chill 6 to 12 hours. Punch dough down, and divide into 4 equal portions; set 1 portion aside. Divide each of the 3 portions into 16 pieces; shape each piece into a ball, and place in well-greased 2¼-inch brioche pans or muffin pans. Make a deep indentation in center of each ball, using a floured index finger.

Divide reserved portion of dough into 48 pieces; shape each piece into a ball. Press 1 ball into each indentation. Cover and let rise in a warm place (85°), free from drafts, 15 to 30 minutes or until brioches are almost doubled in bulk.

Combine egg yolk and water, stirring well; lightly brush top of each brioche. Bake at 375° for 12 minutes or until golden brown, repositioning brioche tops after 3 minutes, if necessary. Remove from pans, and let cool on wire racks. Yield: 4 dozen.

Cinnamon Coffee

1 cup whole Colombian coffee
  beans
1 teaspoon ground cinnamon
2 teaspoons vanilla extract
9 cups water
Cream and sugar to taste

Place whole coffee beans in coffee grinder; process to a medium grind.

Assemble drip coffee maker according to manufacturer's directions. Place ground coffee beans in coffee filter or filter basket; sprinkle with cinnamon and vanilla.

Add water to coffee maker, and brew according to manufacturer's directions. Serve coffee immediately with cream and sugar to taste. Yield: 2 quarts.

Acknowledgments and Credits

Additional Photography/Photo Styling
Beth Maynor/Marjorie Johnston, 78-79, 81, 82-83, 90-91, 93, 95,
132-133, 135, 136, 138-139, 141, 142, 150-151, 153, 155, 162-163,
165, 166-167, 168-169, 171, 172, 173, 192-193, 195, 196-197,
198-199, 201, 203, 204-205, 207, 209, 210-211, 212, 213, 214.
Beth Maynor/Norman Kent Johnson, 30-31, 38, 42-43.

Floral Designs
Jean Condrey, Susan Huff, and Beth Jordan (The King's
    Garden), 39 (left), 69.
Peggy Conway (Overbrook Flowers, Inc.), cover, 126-127.
Maloy Love (Mountain Brook Flower Shop), 96-97, 156-157,
    186-187, 188, 228-229.
Dorothy McDaniel (Dorothy McDaniel's Flowers), 25, 39 (right),
    174-175.
Michael Parker (Michael Blooms Designs, Inc.), 114-115.
William H. Whisenant (Park Lane Flowers), 12, 72-73, 76-77,
    90-91, 210-211.

Wine Consultant
Dr. David J. Black (Birmingham Wine Shop)

China, Crystal, Silver Consultant
Minann Boudreaux (Bromberg and Company, Inc.)

Invitations
Stacy Claire Boyd, Birmingham, Alababma

Locations
Mr. Ken Adams
Mr. and Mrs. Robert T. Agnew, Jr.
Dr. and Mrs. Thomas G. Amason, Jr.
Mr. and Mrs. D. Leon Ashford
Mr. and Mrs. Thomas W. Barker, Jr.
Mr. and Mrs. David Byers
Ms. Kris Childs
Mr. and Mrs. Charles T. Clayton
Mr. and Mrs. Charles T. Clayton, Jr.
Mr. and Mrs. Tony Davis
Ms. Cler Doty
Mr. and Mrs. Samuel S. Everette, Jr.
Mr. and Mrs. O. G. Gage
Mr. and Mrs. George T. Gambrill, III
Mr. and Mrs. Emris H. Graham, Jr.
Mr. and Mrs. John L. Hartman, III
Mr. and Mrs. Glenn Ireland, II
Dr. and Mrs. James H. Isobe
Mr. and Mrs. J. Brooke Johnston, Jr.
Dr. and Mrs. Raleigh B. Kent, Jr.
Mr. and Mrs. D. P. Knapp, Jr.
Mr. and Mrs. Gibson Maynor
Mr. and Mrs. Fancis E. McGovern
Dr. and Mrs. Gaylon R. Rogers
Mr. and Mrs. Robert A. Schleusner
Ms. Ellen Stuart
Mr. and Mrs. James A. Todd, Jr.
Dr. and Mrs. Elias C. Watson, III
Dr. and Mrs. Evan H. Zeiger, Jr.
Birmingham Botanical Gardens
Springhouse Antiques
The Wynfrey Hotel

Oxmoor House wishes to thank the following Birmingham merchants and individuals:
AABCO Rents, Attic Antiques, Sara Jane Ball, Birmingham Antique Mall, Inc., Birmingham Wholesale Furniture Company, Blue and
White Shops, Inc., Bridges Antiques, Bromberg and Company, Inc., Christine's, Julie Clarke, Cook Store of Mountain Brook, The
Dande-Lion, The Elegant Earth, Frankie Engel Antiques, The Holly Tree, Inc., King's House Antiques and Oriental Rugs, Leaf 'N
Petal, Leslie, Joyce Lichtenstein, Little Hardware, Macy's, Maralyn Wilson Gallery, Mary Adams Antiques, Mountain Brook Citgo,
Nelson's, Pier I Imports, The Pink Tulip, Plant Odyssey, Presents Perfect, Rich's, Rogers Trading Company, Roy Bridges Jeep
Dealer, Simonton's, Charlie Thigpen, Toni Tully, Turner Rental, Ventura Import, Wardemond Galleries, Weeds 'N Things.

Recipe Index

Subject Index

EVENT _____

DATE _____

TIME _____

The Party Planner

PLACE _____

NUMBER OF GUESTS _____

STYLE/THEME _____

MENU	RECIPE SOURCES & GARNISHES	THINGS TO DO
APPETIZERS:		ONE WEEK BEFORE:
SOUP/SALAD:		3 DAYS BEFORE:
ENTREE:		THE DAY BEFORE:
SIDE DISHES:		
BREADS:		ON THE DAY:
DESSERT:		
BEVERAGES/WINES:		LAST MINUTE:

GUEST LIST/R.S.V.P.	NOTES